THE
VICTORIAN
COOKERY
BOOK

Kitchen of the Reform Club, London
[*photo*: Radio Times Hulton Picture Library]

THE VICTORIAN COOKERY BOOK

Edited
with an Introduction
by Gordon Grimley

TRANSATLANTIC ARTS, INC.
Sole Distributor For North America
P. O. Box 6086
ALBUQUERQUE, NM 87197 U.S.A.

Abelard-Schuman *London*

ERRATA

Page 51, line 4:
    CHÂTEAUBRIANI to read CHÂTEAUBRIANT

Page 72, penultimate line:
    "chaufroid" to read "chaudfroid"

ISBN 0 200 72047 3

Made and printed in Great Britain by
The Garden City Press Limited
Letchworth, Hertfordshire SG6 1JS

ABELARD-SCHUMAN LIMITED
450 Edgware Road, London W2
24 Market Square, Aylesbury, Buckinghamshire

CONTENTS

INTRODUCTION

If the lives of a people are reflected in their eating habits – and those of millions today are reflected in the fact that they subsist at starvation level – then this choice compendium of late Victorian fare should be viewed with a little caution. For the greater part it mirrors only the living standards of a relatively small and 'privileged' part of the population of the middle and upper classes in the last third of the nineteenth century, when just under half of the working population of Britain were forced to exist on an average weekly family income of about nineteen shillings – that is, below a minimum subsistence level, which Seebohm Rowntree calculated in 1899 as 21s 8d (£1.08) for a couple with three children.

Most of the people who lived in the style which the majority of these fascinating dishes indicate, employed what might be seen as a sub-culture of servants, whose numbers had risen by 1871 to nearly one and a half million – not including hotel and restaurant staffs or even private coachmen, who themselves numbered 16,000. Even so, the servants represented a mere sector of what E. J. Hobsbawm has called 'a working class stunned and debilitated by a century of industrialism'. Forty per cent of the volunteers at the beginning of the Boer War were rejected as unfit. Many of them were farm labourers whose average weekly wage was only ten shillings (50p) when cottage rents could cost up to half a crown (12½p) a week and butter 1s 4d (7p) a pound. Even Alexis Soyer, the immortal and great-hearted French chef, who reigned for ten years in the elaborate kitchens he himself designed at the new Reform Club, and whose masterpieces included a 'hundred guinea dish' for a banquet for Victoria and Albert, headed a public subscription for soup kitchens for the poor. He also volunteered for the Crimea in order to try to make the soldiers' rations more palatable.

French cooks coming to Britain during and after the Revolution had a considerable influence on the extravagant nature of Victorian dishes. Mrs Beeton's ideas were much affected, as she said, by her first visits to France; besides, French chefs had fantastic traditions of perfection – Vatel, the King's *maître d'hôtel*, is said to have committed suicide when he found that the fish was arriving too late for a royal banquet. Lord Albemarle's pastrycook requested his master to have the ceiling of the dining room raised in order that it could accommodate a middle dish masterpiece eighteen feet high.

Cookery books abounded in Victorian England. 'The last new cookery book published in this country proclaims that it contains 10,000 receipts,' complains Kettner in his *Book of the Table* (London 1877), and as he rightly said, 'Who wants 10,000 prescriptions when most of us get on all our lives with a few dozen good dishes, and where the fancies of an epicure are limited to a few score?' Cookery schools were also fashionable, for the Great Exhibition of 1851 had presented the public with a notable onslaught of domestic wares, including gas mantles, a knife-cleaning machine, enamelled frying pans, and a gas cooker to provide meals for a hundred people at a time. By 1859, as Mrs Beeton observed in the first edition of her own cookery book, gas cooking was scarcely a novelty for the well-to-do: 'Many establishments both large and small have been fitted with apparatus for cooking by this mode, which undoubtedly exhibits some advantages. Thus the heat may be more regularly supplied to the substance cooking, and the operation is essentially a clean one, because there can be no cinders or other dirt to be provided for . . . Besides this, it may be said that culinary operations are reduced to a certainty.'

Foremost among the commercially-tuned culinary experts was Mrs A. B. Marshall, whose School of Cookery occupied two

View of Mrs. A. B. Marshall's Class Room during the progress of an Entire Dinner Lesson on May 6, 1887.

A full Report of the Menu and Dinner was given in the 'QUEEN' newspaper of May 27, 1887.

The World.—'On Entire Dinner Lesson Days the School of Cookery, in Mortimer Street, assumes the appearance of a culinary parliament. For seven consecutive hours Mrs. Marshall continues to arrest the attention of cooks and mistresses while she initiates them into the mysteries of dainty dishes.'

The Queen.—'Go and see for yourself at this School what properly managed cookery is like. Mrs. Marshall must be doing a grand work, for pupils seem literally to pass through her hands by thousands.'

Over Two Hundred Newspapers, and Thousands of Testimonials from Pupils have praised Mrs. A. B. Marshall's work.

SEND FOR FULL PROSPECTUS.

adjoining houses at 30–32 Mortimer Street in the West End of London: 'On entire Dinner Lesson Days,' her advertisement proclaimed, 'the School assumes the appearance of a culinary Parliament. For seven consecutive hours Mrs Marshall continues to arrest the attention of cooks and mistresses while she initiates them into the mysteries of dainty dishes.' Like other Victorian entrepreneurs, Mrs Marshall was a considerable publicist and business woman. Part of her Mortimer Street premises formed virtually a small department store where an entire range of kitchen equipment could be bought, including kitchen ranges and gas cookers. Numerous culinary preparations were sold under her name and label, and her public 'practical lectures' on cookery were frequent. Her name appeared under patent on many kitchen items, and a weekly magazine, *The Table*, also originated from her address.

Mrs Marshall would not, however, have been popular with dieticians such as John Smith, who in his *Vegetable Cookery* (1866) felt that 'all food in a hot state, whether solid or liquid, should be avoided, as it acts injuriously on the teeth, debilitates the stomach and, through it, every other portion of the animal system . . . An elegant taste will be more rationally employed in rendering a plain, wholesome and nutritious dish inviting, than in embellishing trifles, custards and other rich productions which are more adapted to create indigestion than to satisfy a normal appetite.'

The kitchen was the hub of the well-to-do Victorian household. Even up to the first third of the present century, relatively small town and suburban houses were built with kitchen, scullery and larder of 'working size'. Increasing land values were not the primary factor in drastically reducing kitchen size after the 1950s. Joints, hams, tubs of butter and all the hardware impedimenta of earlier kitchens needed far more space than today's tinned, ready-mixed and frozen foods, slimline cookers, fridges and central heating units which can be placed elsewhere in the house. Television also materially helped to swing the domestic focal point from one part of the house to another.

New, the kitchen of even a moderately-sized Victorian house must have looked a magnificent affair, its altar the iron or steel range which burned throughout the year, providing hot water for the house as well as the means for cooking, roasting and baking. Blackleaded daily, its edges, if of steel, also had to be scoured with

emery paper, and a normal household model would contain up to three ovens, each with its own thick door and with numerous holes in the great top plate for saucepans, frying pans and kettle. Flanking it on either side would be two large cupboards containing linen and cutlery. Opposite was the dresser holding all but the best crockery: the plates and saucers on shelves and the cups and jugs dangling on hooks. The variety of crockery was endless, including such nowadays 'antique' curiosities as vegetable dishes, huge meat

Top to bottom: Border moulds; copper skillets
or sugar pans; boiler and two copper basins

platters, and a regiment of meat covers in china or steel, graduated in size to cover everything from a few chops to the largest sirloins of beef.

As the engine room of the house, the kitchen required both a talent for organisation and an enthusiasm for elbow grease; the cook possessed the former and, in a house of reasonable size, instilled the latter into the cook-maids, kitchen-maids and scullerymaids who lived under her stern eye: what Tennyson called 'the sooty yoke of vassalage'. Washing up hundreds of dishes after a large dinner party, to say nothing of the ensuing utensil, oven and kitchen cleaning and polishing, must have represented a dreary and seemingly endless task for a girl whose working hours were invariably from 6 a.m. to 10 p.m. and whose annual wage would be between £10 and £20 according to her rank or years of service. In choosing such overworked vassals, *The Young Housewife's Daily Assistant* recommended that 'in taking the character, questions should be put as to the morals, habits, cleanliness, capability and health of the servant, and there should be no hesitation or prevarication in the answers.... It will be found a good plan to write down the daily work of each servant and the

Top to bottom: Travelling stewpans; cases for transporting broth; freezing bucket for ices and iced soufflés

hours for doing it, as well as the days on which extra cleaning is required. The hours for rising, meals, retiring and all matters on which order and comfort depend [the mistress's, of course, and not the servants'—Ed.] should also be written out.... All stores are regulated by receipts, as each contains the exact quantity required.'

If servants were not trusted, neither were tradesmen. Every good kitchen had its pair of scales and all deliveries to the house were weighed on receipt. Cooks, of course, were not above disposing of surplus 'oddments': dripping was a great favourite to be sold surreptitiously at the back door before the family were up and about, and bones also fetched money.

Meat was ever the staple food, and the proportion of the budget spent on it is well evidenced by the following estimate of monthly expenditure in *The Young Housewife's Daily Assistant* for a middle-class family without children and with one or two servants:

Baker and Confectioner	£1. 0. 0½d
Butterman and Cheesemonger	1. 17. 8d
Butcher and Pork Butcher	4. 0. 1d
Fishmonger and Poulterer	1. 14. 6d
Greengrocer and Fruiterer	1. 5. 6½d
Grocer and Oilman	1. 14. 9d
Dairyman	9. 5d

Moulds various

As Kettner remarked, 'The dinner of the Englishman, far more than that of foreigners, implies a large joint of meat which afterwards has to be eaten cold. There is cold meat at breakfast, cold meat at luncheon, cold meat at supper, cold meat all day, which is eaten with pickles for lack of a good sauce.' A normal Sunday joint for a middle-class couple was of about 9lb, which did not include provision for the servants whose food would be listed curtly under the single word, *Kitchen*.

Dinner was the principal meal for the well-to-do in the social round. 'Luncheon,' said *Manners and Tone of Good Society* (1873),

> although occupying a prominent place in the round of hospitalities, is nevertheless an unceremonious, an inconsequent meal, to which invitations are never issued formally by invitation cards, unless some special reason existed for giving a large luncheon party, in which case it would rank as an enter-

Safe or cold-closet

> tainment. . . . Luncheon is served either *à la Russe* (buffet) or not, according to the inclination, although as a rule the joint is served from the buffet or side table, while the entrées, game or poultry would be placed on the table before the host or hostess. The sweets, fruit, etc., would be placed on the table also, as would be wine in decanters, sherry and claret being the usual wine drunk at a luncheon. . . . The cover does not include either a table spoon or a fish knife, as soup and fish are seldom given at luncheon, unless the latter is served in the form of dressed fish,

or mayonnaise, when it should be eaten with an ordinary dinner
fork. . . . As at dinner, it is the duty of the hostess to give the
signal for leaving the room, which she does by attracting the
attention of the lady of highest rank present by means of a smile
and a bow, rising at the same time from her seat.

Five o'clock teas, as they were known, often interpolated themselves between luncheon and dinner, and one can imagine that on
high days when all three meals were to be prepared, or even two,
the cook must have required the planning genius of a general. The
'usual refreshments' at such teas were sherry, champagne-cup,
claret cup, ices, fruit, fancy biscuits, cakes, potted game sand-
wiches, and endless other fripperies. But luncheons and five o'clock
teas were as nothing to dinner-parties which 'rank first among all
entertainments, being of more frequent occurrence, and having
more social significance, and being more appreciated by society than
any other form of entertainment.' At least the cook had good
notice, for invitations to such ceremonies – they can be called no
less – were issued twenty-one to fourteen days before the event,
the menus being handwritten in French by the mistress of the
house and ranged along the table. The elaboration of both dishes
and menus often created an enormous sense of expectancy and
anxiety for the hostess. The last half-hour before a dinner party
could, as Mrs Beeton said, be an ordeal of torture.

Ceremony at table was encouraged by Continental writers such as
Urbain-Dubois whose mammoth and beautifully-printed *Cosmo-
politan Cookery* was published in translation by Longmans (1872)
with 378 fine illustrations. The author's quasi-scientific approach
was indicated by his subtitle, *Popular Studies*, and his instructions
on eating which read rather like a manual of golf technique:

Taking one's repasts in society, whether at home or at the tables
of others, is an act of no less real import than all the other
manifestations of decorum and urbanity. . . . In order to eat at
one's ease, and without automatic stiffness, one must first be
seated commodiously, and perpendicularly, neither too high, nor
too low; the chest upright, at an equal distance from the back
of the chair and from the table. On the left of the plate there
should be a solid fork, rather heavy than light; on the right, the
spoon and knife, the latter having a broad blade rounded at the
extremity.

When the hands are not occupied with carving or conveying the food to the mouth, they may be reposing on the edge of the table, but only as far as the wrist. When about to eat (with the exception of soup which is always absorbed by holding the spoon with the right hand), or to cut food that is on the plate, the fork ought to be used with the left hand, the points or prongs turned downwards, and pressed on with the extended forefinger, to maintain it in an almost horizontal position, and not in a perpendicular position. . . .

Movable hot-closet

Of the school of 'la crème de la crème', Urbain Dubois it was who stated that 'young men cannot too carefully make themselves acquainted with the experiences of competent men for meditating and seriously studying the composition of bills of fare; above all, they must never forget that a bill of fare, well composed and ingeniously executed, has more than once altered the destiny of a cook. . . . The matter of composing a bill of fare is a serious thing, never to be undertaken by a cook, but with great reserve and after mature reflection.'

Not a few Victorian housewives about to launch themselves on the social world must have trembled at that and fled back to Mrs Beeton, Mrs Marshall and others, just as housewives of today may be found nervously thumbing otherwise scarcely-opened cookery books if a 'particular occasion' is imminent. Tinned food was not completely unknown to the people of the later nineteenth century: canned meat was reaching Britain in the late 1870s from the USA, where it had been developed by P. G. Armour. Unappetising at first, but also inexpensive, it provided a change of fare for the less well-to-do. Apples represented practically the only fresh fruit which the British working people could afford until the 1870s when, with the growth of the Co-Ops, the first major

Closet for a drawing-room

signs of change began to appear in the supply of consumer markets. Fish and chip shops also made their first appearance in this period, probably in the North of England. Hot pies were always of course to be purchased from street vendors.

One sidelight of Victorian cookery which emerges is the attitude held towards animals generally. A Victorian middle- or upper-class person did not quail at the sight of a pie decorated with the heads of larks, nor did he or she feel squeamish, as we would today, about the appearance on the table of a salmon complete with head. Turtles were bought alive and killed as required: 'Wait until the turtle pokes out its head and then sever it quickly with a sharp knife,' said one cookery manual calmly. It was all part of the great orgiastic ceremony of stomach-filling, with preparations such as Page Woodcock's Wind Pills waiting in the background, the whole concealed and disguised under a fine top dressing of humourless pomposity provided by people like Urbain Dubois and others.

Nevertheless, it may be that Western society generally will yet have cause to look back on the reign of that most domestic monarch, Queen Victoria, as representing the last great age of cooking, for if one concentrates sufficiently on a subject (as any Victorian writer might have said), and if it is attended with sufficient time and thoroughness, the results will be good. Bolstered by money denied to the greater number of their own people, the Victorians whose culinary art is typified here, had the time for this. Never, perhaps, will one now know the true delight of savoury fish pie; rarely – and certainly not commercially – will one encounter the rich, crumbling delight of their deep, platter-sized fruit cakes; and just as rarely will you find a deep-bowl, thick-crusted meat pudding that is anything but a pallid echo of the Victorian wonder of its kind.

My thanks are due to Cassandra Carter for compiling the Glossary.

G.G.

SNACKS
&
BREAKFAST
DISHES

BUBBLE AND SQUEAK

Take some thinly cut slices of cold boiled salt beef (fat and lean) and sprinkle over it a very little coralline pepper; put a piece of butter or clean beef dripping into a sauté or frying pan, make it hot, then put the slices of beef into it, and fry them on both sides till a pretty golden colour; then take up and put the pieces of meat between two plates and keep them hot over boiling water till ready to dish up. Have a nice fresh cabbage plainly boiled and pressed from the water; chop it up finely on a clean board, then put it into the pan in which the beef was fried and fry it for about five minutes; turn it out in the centre of a hot dish on which it is to be served and arrange the fried slices of beef round, and serve very hot.

SAVOURY PORRIDGE

Oatmeal one or two tablespoonfuls, onions two or three ounces, milk one pint, butter a quarter of an ounce, pepper and salt one teaspoonful. Boil the onions in two waters; when tender, shred

them fine, and add them to the boiling milk; sprinkle in the oatmeal, add the butter, pepper, and salt; boil ten to fifteen minutes,
pour it into soup plates, and serve with sippets. Instead of onions,
grated cheese may be stirred in with the oatmeal. Cheese, with
Indian meal or semolina, forms also another variety of polenta,
an Italian dish. For sweet porridge, add sugar, raisins, currants,
etc., instead of the onions and pepper.

THE QUEEN'S TOASTED CHEESE –
RECEIPT FROM THE ROYAL LODGE, WINDSOR

Half a pound of cheese; three tablespoonfuls of ale; one small
glass of Champagne.

Grate half a pound of cheese very fine, and add to it three
tablespoonfuls of ale and a small glass of Champagne. Mix it well
in a silver dish over a lamp for ten minutes, and serve it in the
dish as hot as possible, with a plate of thin toast.

MOCK CRAB – SAILOR FASHION

A large slice of Gloucester cheese; a teaspoonful of mustard, the
same of vinegar; pepper and salt to taste.

Cut a slice of Gloucester cheese rather thin, but of good size
round. Mash it up with a fork to a paste, mix it with vinegar,
mustard, and pepper. It has a great flavour of crab.

RAMAKINS

Two eggs; one teaspoonful of flour; two ounces of melted butter;
two ounces of grated cheese; two tablespoonfuls of cream.

Mix a teaspoonful of flour with two ounces of grated cheese,
two ounces of melted butter, two tablespoonfuls of cream, and

two well-beaten eggs. Stir all together, and bake it in small tins. You may add a little cayenne pepper if you please.

TO MAKE BUTTER

In order to make butter well, it is necessary that the vessels in which the milk is kept be sweet and clean, and the milk-room or cellar cool and airy in summer.

Large tin pans are mostly used for milk, the broadest are the best, allowing a greater surface for the cream to rise.

Vessels in which milk is kept, after being emptied, must first be washed in cold water to take off all the milk, and any remains of cream, then fill them with scalding hot water, which must be sufficed to remain until nearly cold. One pan may be turned over another, which is filled with hot water, for a few minutes, then change their relative positions, pouring the water from one to another; this will require less time and water than the other way. Lastly, wash them well in the water and turn them upside down in the sun. Tin milk pails are best, being most easily kept sweet. White, or hard wood pails are generally used, and must be well washed in cold water and then scalded the same as tin pans. Occasionally, scour both pails and pans with soft soap and sand, and afterwards scald them, rinse them in hot water, and dry them in the sun, or by a fire. Or, instead of scalding the milk tins and other vessels, as above directed, have a large vessel of boiling water, and having first washed them in cold water (turning them round that every part may get its due), let them remain in for a few minutes, then wipe them dry and set them by for use; their own heat will assist the drying.

Milk strainers are tin basins with a fine sieve at the bottom, or with a ring by which to fasten a linen cloth over a bottomless basin. The ring and cloth must be taken off every time it is used, and first washed in cold water; allow it to remain in the water whilst washing the tins, then wash it out, pour scalding water in it, and lastly, rinse it in cold water and hang it to dry.

A small frame or ladder is wanted to lay across the pan and support the strainer whilst the milk is poured through.

For taking the cream from the milk, a short-handle tin skimmer or shell is used. A stone jar or pot is best for keeping cream. There should never be more than three days' gatherings for a churning; too long keeping will make bitter butter. Wash the jar in cold water, and scald and dry as directed for tins.

Wooden ware churns are the most commonly used. The old-fashioned barrel churn is best for small churnings; a larger sort, in which the dasher is suspended and moved back and forth, instead of up and down, is less tiresome; the churn is to be kept sweet and clean in the same manner as the other vessels, exposing the inside to the heat of the sun until thoroughly dry, after each time washing.

A wooden tray and ladle are also necessary for receiving and working the butter after it is made.

Care is necessary that the churning is neither too fast nor too slowly performed. The dashes should be continued at intervals of about a second between them, and steadily, until the butter has come, when a slower and more gentle motion is desirable.

Scald the tray and ladle, then fill it with cold water until the butter is made.

After the butter is fairly gathered, take it from the buttermilk with the ladle, pressing it against the sides of the churn to free it from the milk; having thrown the water from the tray put the butter in, pour cold water over to cover it, and set it in a cool place for half an hour to harden it; then with the ladle work all the milk from it, changing the water until it is clear; it is best to have ice water in summer if possible.

To each pound of butter put a small tablespoonful of fine salt, and a small teaspoonful of fine white sugar; work it nicely into the butter and make it in rolls, or pack it in wooden or stone vessels; put in a piece of muslin and a cover to keep the butter from the air.

Butter should be made and kept in a cool cellar or ice house; this direction is particularly for summer, when it must be done in the coolest part of the day, and the coolest possible place. Cold water poured in occasionally in small quantities, at the dasher, will make the butter come better in summer.

In warm weather milk is generally ready for skimming after twenty-four hours standing, when the cream is wanted for butter. If you churn in winter pour boiling water into the churn, cover it, and let it remain until ready to put in the cream, at which time throw it out. Winter churning should be done in a moderately warm room.

TO SCALD CREAM AS IN THE WEST OF ENGLAND

To stand in the winter twenty-four hours; twelve in summer.

Strain the milk into large shallow pans about three or four inches deep, and let it stand for twenty-four hours; then place the pan very carefully upon a hot plate, or slow fire, to heat gently, taking care it does not boil, or there will be a skin instead of a cream upon the milk. As soon as the cream forms a ring round the pan, and the undulations on the surface look thick, it is done; then remove from the fire into the dairy, and let it remain for twenty-four hours, or if it be in cold weather, thirty-six; then skim it for use. The butter usually made in Devonshire of cream thus prepared is very firm and good.

KEDGEREE OF FISH

Put a gill of thick cream into a stewpan with one and a half ounces of butter and season with a pinch of salt and a tiny dust of coralline pepper; boil up all together, then mix with six large tablespoonfuls of any cold cooked fish, two large tablespoonfuls of plainly boiled rice, and four hard-boiled eggs that are cut up in small pieces; just let the kedgeree boil up, and then turn out on to a hot dish in a pile. Serve for a breakfast dish.

SOUPS

THICK TOMATO SOUP

Wash and dry two ounces of white mushrooms, and put them in a stewpan, with two ounces of butter, four large onions sliced, two leeks, three or four strips of celery, a good bunch of herbs, one saltspoonful of mignonette pepper, a teaspoonful of French mustard, and a good dust of coralline pepper. Fry them together for about twenty minutes, stirring occasionally, then add eight or ten large tomatoes (fresh are best) sliced, the juice of one large lemon, and three ounces of crême de riz; mix to this two and a half quarts of stock, put it on the stove, and let it simmer gently for about an hour; then pour the stock from the vegetables, and pound these in the mortar; replace it in the stock, pass the whole through a tammy or sieve, and heat it in the bain-marie. For each quart of soup take the raw yolk of three eggs, and mix them in a basin with one and a half gills of warm cream, one ounce of butter, and a tiny pinch of castor sugar, stir in the bain-marie until it thickens, colour it with a few drops of carmine, and strain it into the tureen. Serve with croûtons of bread, handed round on a plate on a napkin, or tiny quenelles served in the soup.

SOUP A LA SANTÉ

Put into a stewpan two ounces of butter, half a pound of lean ham or bacon, two pounds of leg of beef tied up with a string, any chopped-up game or poultry bones, raw or cooked, a dust of coralline pepper, two large onions, two carrots, half a stick of celery, one large leek all sliced, and six or eight peppercorns. Fry all together with the lid on the pan for twenty minutes, occasionally shaking the pan to prevent anything sticking to the bottom, then pour into the pan about four quarts of stock, bring it steadily to the boil, keep it skimmed, and let it simmer for about four hours, then remove the beef, strain off the stock, let it get cold, remove the fat, and clarify the soup, then put it in the bain-marie. Blanch some carrot, turnip, celery, leek and lettuce, cut all into shreds about one and a half inches long, and drain them; melt two ounces of butter in a stewpan, lay in the shredded vegetables, and fry them until of a very pale colour, then add sufficient clarified stock to cover them, and boil gently until the vegetables are quite tender, and all the butter has been skimmed off, then add them to the soup before serving. Cut some of the beef taken from the stock into pieces the size of a filbert, warm them in a little stock, and add them to the soup. The rest of the beef can be used as a dish separately. The shredded vegetables may be taken from those used for the stock. Serve with croûtons separately or in the soup.

POT AU FEU

For eight or ten persons take four pounds of rump of beef, or the top of the leg (the meat must be perfectly fresh for this soup), and tie the meat into a nice shape with tape; place three or four pounds of fresh beef or veal bones in the bottom of either an earthenware or very clean tinned stewpan, lay the meat on top of the bones and add six quarts of cold water and a good dessertspoonful of salt; this must come most gently to the boil, and any scum arising must be carefully removed, and a little cold water (about one pint in all) frequently added to cause the scum to rise freely. The soup should be of a golden amber colour when ready to serve. When thoroughly skimmed add to the stock two freshly cleaned carrots, one large turnip, two leeks, a small stick of celery, one parsnip, a bunch of herbs, four onions (one stuck with six cloves), and about twenty peppercorns, black and white, the herbs and spice all being tied up in a piece of muslin. The vegetables must be put in by degrees, so as not to reduce the temperature of the stock too much at once, and after the vegetables are all in, the stock must not be allowed to boil fast. Skim it well, then partly cover the pan and leave it to cook, simmering very gently on the side of the stove for about six hours. Then take up the meat carefully, remove the tape, dish it and garnish with some of the vegetables, also a purée of spinach, or, if liked, fresh braised cabbage may be used. Strain the stock after skimming off the fat, and send it to the table quite boiling with some of the vegetables cut into neat squares, and round pieces of the crust of French roll prepared as for croûte au pot, either served in the soup or handed round on a plate. A pinch of sugar, and a very little salt, if needed, may be added to the soup before serving.

PURÉE OF ARTICHOKES

Cut two pounds and a half of peeled Jerusalem artichokes in thin slices, add to them two large onions sliced, a little celery, a bunch of herbs (thyme, parsley and a bayleaf), and fry all together in two ounces of butter in a sauté pan until a pale golden colour, add four ounces of crême de riz; then put them in a saucepan with two and a half quarts of new milk or light stock, and cook for about two hours, keeping it well skimmed; pass it through a tammy or fine hair sieve, put it in a pan on the bain-marie to keep quite hot, and just before serving add to it a pint of single cream, a dust of coralline pepper, and a tiny pinch of salt. Little squares of stale bread, fried a pale golden colour in good dripping or clarified butter, and dished up on a napkin or dish-paper, may be served with this soup.

THICK OXTAIL SOUP

Cut the oxtail up in lengths by the joints, the larger pieces may be subdivided into four or five pieces; put these, with a pinch of salt, into enough cold water to cover them, and bring gently to the boil; strain off the water and wash the meat well, put it into a clean stewpan, with about six or seven pints of ordinary cold stock, or water if you have no stock, four onions, sticking half a dozen cloves into one of them, a few strips of celery, three carrots, one turnip, two leeks, a good bunch of herbs, such as basil, marjoram, thyme, parsley, bayleaf, all tied up together, with about two blades of mace and about twelve black and white peppercorns, a good dust of coralline pepper, and a few drops of carmine; let the whole boil up gently, then skim, and simmer for about four hours; when the meat is tender, strain the stock through a hair sieve, and pick the meat away from the vegetables. Remove all the fat from the stock, put it in a pan, and thicken it with two small tablespoonfuls of cornflour, which is first mixed with a little cold stock. Take all the vegetables and pound them, and add them to the soup as soon as it is boiled up again; pass the whole through the tammy; make hot in the bain-marie, add the pieces of meat, allowing two or three pieces per person; a little sherry may be added if liked, and any pieces of the meat left over can be used up as an entrée.

OYSTER SOUP

Take twenty-four oysters: remove the fins or beards and tendons, and put all together – oysters, fins and tendons – to simmer for ten minutes in their own liquor, along with a small sole. The sole, the fins and the tendons are then to be pounded in a mortar and passed into a stewpan, with the liquor of the oysters, a quart of water, or still better fish stock, a faggot of sweet-herbs, and a few peppercorns. Let it boil for fifteen or twenty minutes, and then work into it an ounce of butter kneaded into flour one ounce, till the flour be thoroughly cooked. The soup can then be strained into a tureen; thickened with a leason composed of one yolk of egg and two tablespoonfuls of cream; seasoned with cayenne and salt; and finally populated with the oysters.

A SIMPLE PRAWN OR SHRIMP SOUP

One hundred prawns or twice as many shrimps; a quarter of a pound of butter; two French rolls; one quart of good beef gravy, or fish stock; a bunch of herbs; a little vingear and water; a little pepper and salt.

Pick the prawns or shrimps, and then pound them in a quarter of a pound of butter. Pound the shells and boil them in a little vinegar and water; strain a little of this liquor over the prawns in a stewpan, add two French rolls and a quart of good beef gravy or fish stock; put it to stew for an hour, but take care that it does not boil; rub it through a tammy; add a few whole prawns; warm it again and serve.

GREEN PEA SOUP

Three cos lettuces; three cucumbers; one pint of green peas; a sprig of mint; one onion; a little parsley; four ounces of fresh butter; half a pint of thin gravy.

Cut up three cos lettuces, pare and slice three cucumbers, add a pint of young green peas, a sprig of mint, one onion, and a little parsley. Put all into a stewpan with a quarter of a pound of fresh butter, and let it stew half an hour, then pour in half a pint of thin gravy, stew it for two hours, thicken it with a little lump of butter rolled in flour and serve.

RABBIT SOUP (EXPENSIVE)

Four rabbits; six pounds of shin of beef; four onions; three carrots; one head of celery; two turnips; a teaspoonful of white pepper; seven quarts of water; a little salt and cayenne; one pint of cream to every three pints of soup.

Put the rabbits, beef, onions, carrots, turnips, celery, and a teaspoonful of white pepper into a stewpan with seven quarts of water, let it boil gently five or six hours, adding a little salt and cayenne; strain, and let it stand until cold; take off the fat, and to every three pints of soup put a pint of cream. The fleshy parts of the rabbits should be taken off and pounded, as soon as they are tender, and this pounded meat is to be added to the soup before it is served. Veal, or any other good stock, will do as well as beef, if more convenient.

AN ECONOMICAL WHITE SOUP

A knuckle of veal; one slice of lean ham; two onions; a bunch of thyme; a few cloves; half a blade of mace; four ounces of pounded almonds; half a pint of cream; one egg; water in proportion to the meat.

Take a knuckle of veal, separate it into several pieces, and put it into a stewpan with a slice of *lean* ham, two onions, a bunch of thyme, a few cloves, and half a blade of mace. Pour in sufficient water for the quantity of soup required, and let it stew for twelve or fourteen hours, until the stock is as rich as the ingredients can make it. When sufficiently stewed, set it to cool, and carefully remove the fat; add to it four ounces of almonds blanched and pounded; let it boil slowly again, and thicken it with half a pint of cream and a well-beaten egg. It should boil slowly for half an hour, and then serve it.

MOCK TURTLE SOUP [1]

Ten pounds of shin of beef; a bunch of sweet herbs; two onions; half a calf's head; a very little flour; a little pounded mace and cloves; two spoonfuls of mushroom ketchup; pepper and salt; a glass of sherry; and some egg-balls.

Take the shin of beef, cut it into small pieces, and fry the lean part a light brown; put the rest of the beef into a stewpan with boiling water, and stew it for eight hours, with a bunch of sweet herbs, and two onions. When cold, take off the fat. Then get half a calf's head with the skin on, half boil it, and cut it into small square pieces, put it into the soup, and let it stew together till quite tender. Add the browned lean shin of beef, thicken it with a very little flour, add the mace, cloves, and mushroom ketchup, and a little soy. Season it with pepper and salt to your taste. Put in it a few egg-balls, and a wineglass of sherry.

MOCK TURTLE SOUP [2]

Have ready half of a small calf's head with the skin on, two pounds of lean veal, two pounds of very fresh lean beef, half a pound of mild lean ham, three onions, a head of celery, two large carrots, one turnip, a small bunch of mixed sweet herbs, a bunch of fresh parsley, three sage leaves, garlic, spice, sugar, anchovy-sauce, soy, butter, baked flour, a gill of Marsala, two wineglassfuls of Madeira or rich brown sherry, lemons, etc. Peel, scrape, wash, slice and fry the vegetables to a pale brown colour in a quarter of a pound of butter. Put the veal and the beef into an iron pot with a pint of cold water, and let it stand by the side of the fire for an hour, to draw out the gravy; then put in the vegetables, the herbs, ham, six peppercorns, four cloves, a blade of mace, a piece of garlic the size of a pea, a teaspoonful of salt, a tablespoonful of loaf sugar, the head, skin uppermost, and four quarts of cold water. Boil up quickly; skim. Put in the Marsala, and simmer gently for two hours, skimming frequently. Take out the head, pull out the bones, and trim off all the rough pieces; put the meat between two dishes, with a heavy weight on the upper one, and let it get cold. Put the bones and trimmings back in the pot, and simmer for four hours, skimming constantly. Knead a quarter of a pound of fresh butter with five tablespoonfuls of flour, baked till slightly browned, two grains of cayenne, a teaspoonful of flour of mustard, a salt-

. .

spoonful of white pepper, and a saltspoonful of salt. Stir this into the soup. Add a dessertspoonful of soy and a teaspoonful of anchovy-sauce. Boil for a quarter of an hour, then strain through a fine sieve. Cut the meat of the head into inch-square pieces; put it into the soup, add the strained juice of a lemon; simmer for twenty minutes. Put in the Madeira or sherry, and serve immediately. Cut lemons and cayenne should be handed.

POOR MAN'S SOUP

Two quarts of water; four spoonfuls of beef dripping; an ounce and a half of butter; a pint basinful of raw potatoes; a young cabbage; a little salt.

Put two quarts of water in a stewpan, and when boiling throw in four spoonfuls of beef dripping, an ounce and a half of butter and a pint basinful of raw potatoes sliced, and let them boil one hour. Pick a young cabbage, leaf by leaf, or the heart of a white cabbage, but do not chop it small, throw it in and let it boil ten minutes, or till the cabbage be done to taste, though when boiled fast and green it eats much better. Season it with a little salt, and throw over thin slices of bread in a tureen.

COTTAGE SOUP BAKED

A pound of meat; two onions; two carrots; two ounces of rice; a pint of whole peas; pepper and salt; a gallon of water.

Cut the meat into slices, put one or two at the bottom of an earthen jar or pan, lay on it the onions sliced, then put meat again, then the carrots sliced. Soak the pint of peas all the previous night, put them in with one gallon of water. Tie the jar down and put it in a hot oven for three or four hours.

BONE STOCK FOR SOUP

Bones of any meat which has been dressed, as sirloin bone, leg of mutton bone, etc.; two scraped carrots; one stick of celery; enough cold water to cover the bones, or enough of the liquor left from braising meat to cover them; one teaspoonful of salt.

Break the bones into very small pieces, put them into a stewpan with the carrots and celery; cover them with cold water or cold braise liquor, and let it boil quickly till the scum rises; skim it off and throw in some cold water, when the scum will rise again. This must be done two or three times, till the stock is quite clear; then draw the pan from the fire and let it stew for two hours, till all the goodness is extracted from the bones. Strain it off and let it stand all night. The next day take off the grease very carefully, not leaving the least atom on it, and lift it from the sediment at the bottom of the pan. It will then be ready for use.

LETTUCE AND CUCUMBER SOUP

Cabbage lettuces four, cos lettuce one, sorrel one handful, tarragon and chervil a little of each, cucumbers two or three small ones. Wash, dry and cut the lettuces, pare and slice the cucumbers; add butter four ounces. Stir the whole over a slow fire till no liquid remains; add two tablespoonfuls of flour, mix well, and then add gradually two quarts of broth, or water only, and boil; when boiling add a pint of green peas, two teaspoonfuls of sugar, and a little salt and pepper; when the peas are tender, serve.

Alternatively: Cucumbers five or six of a moderate size, cos lettuces six, bread crumbs six ounces, onions four ounces, parsley one ounce, butter four ounces. Pare and slice the cucumbers and onions; dress and cut the lettuces; add the parsley with a little seasoning; put the vegetables in a pan with the butter, and stew them gently for three-quarters of an hour; then pour in two quarts of boiling water, add the breadcrumbs, and let the soup simmer gently for two hours. If too thin, mix a teaspoonful of flour with an ounce of butter, stir it well in, boil ten minutes longer, and add a tablespoonful of tarragon vinegar.

RAVIOLI SOUP

Have in readiness the following articles: A fowl or pheasant, two partridges, three pounds of lean veal, three pounds of lean beef, half a pound of lean ham, two carrots, four onions, one head of celery, four mushrooms, a small bunch of mixed sweet herbs, a laurel leaf and four sprigs of parsley (all tied together), garlic, shallot, butter, flour, eggs, Parmesan cheese, new Neufchâtel cheese, spinach, spice, half a gill of port wine, and a wineglassful of either Madeira or Marsala. Peel and cut up the vegetables and half a clove of garlic. Put them into an iron pot, with six ounces of butter, the beef, ham, and veal, and stand one hour by the fire to brown and extract the gravy. Then put in a quart of warm water, and the birds, breasts uppermost; simmer for an hour. Take out the birds, cut off the meat from the breasts, about three ounces of each, without skin. Put back the carcasses into the pot, add four quarts of warm water, a tablespoonful of soy, a dessertspoonful of loaf sugar, a teaspoonful of salt, a teaspoonful of flour of mustard, a grain of cayenne, a saltspoonful of pepper, a blade of mace, four allspice, three cloves, six peppercorns, and the herbs. Simmer gently, and skim frequently, for five hours.

In the meantime, make the ravioli as follows: Rub two ounces of butter into six ounces of well-dried flour; moisten with two beaten yolks of fresh eggs, and half a gill of water; knead and roll out the paste a quarter of an inch thick, and let it stand in a cool dry place for three or four hours; pound the meat of the breasts, an ounce of lean ham, an ounce of Neufchâtel cheese, the yolks of two hard-boiled eggs, an ounce of cooked spinach, and one shallot. Season with the sixth part of a nutmeg grated, half a saltspoonful of white pepper, a quarter of a saltspoonful of flour of mustard, a teaspoonful of thick anchovy sauce, half a saltspoonful of loaf sugar; add an ounce of butter and a tablespoonful of grated Parmesan cheese. Pound to a smooth paste; mix in the Marsala. Roll out the paste as thin as possible; cut it into two and a half inch squares (about sixteen); brush them over with water; divide the forcemeat into the same number of parts; put one into each square; turn over one corner so as to form small three-cornered puffs; press the edges well round with the thumb to make them adhere; drop them one by one into a saucepan of boiling water with a teaspoonful of salt in it, and boil slowly for seven minutes.

Take them up carefully and drain on a sieve, in the oven, for ten minutes.

Stir into the soup four tablespoonfuls of baked flour and three teaspoonfuls of Parmesan cheese; then strain. Put it into a stewpan; boil up; throw in the ravioli; boil slowly for twenty minutes; add the port wine, and serve immediately, with a dish of grated Parmesan separate.

NB: Leveret or pigeons may be substituted when partridges are not to be had.

VEGETABLES

DRY CURRY OF VEGETABLES

Peel four onions and cut them in tiny dice shapes or thin slices, and put them with two ounces of butter (or fat) in a stewpan and fry together till a nice golden colour, then add a dessertspoonful of curry powder, a saltspoonful of ground ginger, ditto of salt, three red dry chillies pounded, four cloves or a pinch of ground cloves, a pinch of ground cinnamon, a teaspoonful of finely chopped bay-leaf and thyme, the juice of one large lemon, and half a pint of water or stock; cook together till the mixture is quite dry, but taking care that it does not burn, then mix it into about one and a half pints altogether of any nicely cooked vegetables, such as carrots, cauliflowers, turnips, beans, etc.; just mix up all together, and dish in a border of rice made with a quarter of a pound of rice. Serve for luncheon or second course dish.

SOUFFLÉ OF CAULIFLOWER A LA BARONNE

Trim a nice cauliflower, put it to blanch, then rinse it and put it into boiling water with a little salt, and let it cook until tender;

take up again, drain and cut it into neat pieces and place them in a buttered soufflé dish with alternate layers of raw sliced tomatoes; season with a very little salt and coralline pepper, and fill up the dish with a soufflé mixture prepared as below, and sprinkle over with a few browned breadcrumbs; place a few pieces of butter here and there on the top, and bake in a moderate oven for thirty minutes, dish up on a paper with a napkin round, sprinkle it with a little chopped parsley, and serve for second course or luncheon.

MIXTURE FOR CAULIFLOWER SOUFFLÉ

Mix two ounces of butter, one and a half ounces of fine flour, one and a half raw yolks of eggs, tiny dust of coralline pepper, a saltspoonful of salt, with not quite half a pint of cold milk; stir over the fire till it boils, then add three ounces of grated Parmesan cheese and the whites of three eggs that have been whipped stiff, with a pinch of salt, and use.

ARTICHOKE BOTTOMS EN ROBE

Take some cooked artichoke bottoms (these can, if liked, be bought already prepared in tins), season them with a few drops of lemon juice and chopped parsley and coralline pepper; have some very fresh and very small eggs poached, and place one of these eggs on each artichoke bottom; care must be taken that the egg does not break; cover the egg over entirely with a light purée of cooked chicken or white meat, using a bag and plain forcing pipe for this purpose; make the purée of chicken quite smooth over the top with a knife which is occasionally dipped in boiling water, and then stand each artichoke bottom containing the egg and the purée on a little round fried croûton; place these on a baking tin in a moderate oven with a well-greased paper over the top of them, and leave them in the oven for about ten minutes; sprinkle them with a little chopped tongue or ham and parsley; stick a little sprig of tarragon in the top of each, and dish up on dish-paper or napkin, and serve for second course or luncheon dish, or for an entrée.

PURÉE OF CHICKEN OR WHITE MEAT

Pound half a pound of cooked white meat with two tablespoonfuls of thick béchamel sauce, one dessertspoonful of tarragon vinegar, one ounce of butter, a little coralline pepper and salt; when pounded smooth rub the mixture through a coarse hair or fine wire sieve, put into the bain-marie and make quite hot, and use.

POTATOES CRUMBED

Peel and boil the potatoes carefully; when they are cooked, but not broken, split them in halves; season with a little coralline pepper and salt; pour over them a little warm butter, and then dip them in browned breadcrumbs, place them on a buttered tin and cook in a quick oven for about fifteen minutes. Dish up en couronne and serve hot.

MASHED POTATOES BAKED

Boil some peeled potatoes, with a little salt in the water, till they are tender; then drain them, and when quite dry pass them through a wire sieve, or mash them in a saucepan; season with a little coralline pepper and salt, a little warm butter and a little milk, to make them moist; when these are well mixed roll the mixture into a ball, place it on a buttered tin, and draw it up into a loaf or beehive shape with a knife or a fork; sprinkle it over with browned breadcrumbs, made from crusts of bread baked, crushed up, and rubbed through a sieve. Cook the potatoes in the oven for about twenty minutes with a few little pieces of butter placed here and there on them. When a pretty colour dish up, lightly sprinkle a little parsley over, and serve while hot.

TOMATOES A LA NEVILLE

Remove the peel from some small, ripe, sound tomatoes with a sharp pointed knife and open the top parts round the core, then with a small scoop remove the seedy part, and season the inside of the tomatoes with the seasoning used for the artichokes below, and by means of a forcing bag and plain pipe fill them up with a purée of chicken prepared as below; mask over entirely the outside of the tomatoes with aspic cream, garnish the tops with a little ring or star of truffle, and set this to the aspic cream with a little liquid aspic jelly; dish up the tomatoes on cooked artichoke bottoms that are seasoned with a little finely chopped shallot and parsley, or tarragon and chervil, and serve for a second course of luncheon dish, or for ball supper.

CHICKEN PURÉE

For six to eight small tomatoes, take half a pound of cooked chicken, freed from bone and skin, one large tablespoonful of thick cream, one tablespoonful of béchamel sauce, a little salt and coralline pepper, and a teaspoonful of extract of meat; pound all together till smooth, then rub it through a fine hair sieve, and use.

SAVOURY VEGETABLE PIE

Potatoes two pounds, onions two ounces, butter one ounce, water half a pint. Pare and cut the potatoes; put a layer of onions, cut small, between the layers of potatoes; season with pepper and salt; lay the butter at the top in small pieces; pour in the water; cover the whole with paste, and bake.

The onions may be replaced by mushrooms, cut small. Hard-boiled eggs, cut in slices or small pieces, may be distributed between the layers. Half an ounce of tapioca or sago is an improvement; these should be well washed and steeped in cold water before they are added, or they may be reduced to a jelly, and added to the pie when baked. When mushrooms are not used, the flavour may be improved by the addition of a little ketchup, which may either be added when the pie is made, or poured in with a little melted butter, etc., after the pie has been baked. Some add a little celery or powdered sage, sliced turnips, carrots, asparagus, or other vegetables.

HERB PUDDING

Parsley leaves two handfuls, spinach one handful, hearts of lettuces two, mustard and cress one handful (large), a few leaves of white beet, and a small handful of chives.

Wash and boil all the herbs together for three minutes; drain the water from them, then mash and mix them well, adding pepper and salt. Stir in a batter consisting of flour one ounce, thin cream one pint, eggs two. Put the whole in a dish, and cover with a good crust.

SALAD OF VEGETABLES, WITH JELLY

Cut up the heads of some white sprue-asparagus, about two inches long; scrape, and boil them in salted water. Boil also some green sprue-asparagus, a cauliflower in small flowrets, carrots in balls, French beans, flageolet-beans, potatoes with the peel on, celery-roots, and beetroots.

With a part of the green asparagus form a small bundle, which secure in form with a ring of carrot; keep them aside, with a part of the white asparagus, and carrots in balls. Mix the remainder of the vegetables in a kitchen-basin, add a few gherkins, stoned olives, and capers; season, baste with oil and vinegar, in which leave them for ten minutes; drain afterwards, put back into the pan, and thicken with a few tablespoonfuls of mayonnaise with jelly. With this preparation, fill a pyramidal mould, embedded in pounded ice. When the preparation is set, turn it out on a little stand, fixed on the centre of a dish, and take the mould off.

Take the asparagus set by, dip them in half-set jelly, and arrange them upright at the base of the pyramid, applying them against it; above the asparagus place the cauliflowers, then a row of round carrots; repeat a second row of cauliflowers, and above this one, a circle of olives. Set the small bundle of green asparagus on the top, and glaze all the vegetables with half-set aspic. Place all round the edges of the stand a circle of halves of eggs, garnished with a macédoine of small vegetables, of various shades of colour, thickened with aspic jelly. Then surround the base of the stand with jelly-croûtons, and send up separately a boatful of mayonnaise-sauce with eggs.

GREEN SALAD A LA BATELIÈRE

Take some sandwich moulds and line them thinly with aspic jelly, then sprinkle the first and third quarters of the bottoms with coralline pepper or lobster coral which has been passed through a sieve, and the second and fourth quarters with finely chopped tarragon; set this garnish with a few drops of aspic jelly, then sprinkle over with long thin strips of cooked French beans and finely shredded crisp lettuce to fill the moulds, set these with more jelly, and when cold dip them in hot water and turn out; dish them on a border of green salad prepared as below; garnish the salad mixture without the aspic in it, and some nice scallops of cooked lobster may also be arranged in a neat pile in the centre; garnish the dish and round the top of the border with chopped aspic jelly, and sprinkle it here and there with a little coral or coralline pepper and chopped tarragon and chervil. This is a pretty dish for any cold collation, and is a good way to use up any cold lobster.

GREEN SALAD FOR BORDER

Take a handful mixed all together of tarragon, chervil, fennel and parsley, and one sliced shallot; wash these well, and put them into a stewpan with enough cold water to cover them, add a pinch of salt and soda, put it on the stove, and when it comes to the boil strain and press the water from it, then pound these ingredients with six turned olives, two French gherkins, six boned anchovies, one saltspoonful of apple green, one tablespoonful of salad oil, and pass all through a tammy or hair sieve, and then to each one and a half tablespoonfuls of this purée add four tablespoonfuls of thick mayonnaise sauce, a good dust of coralline pepper, a pint and a half of liquid aspic jelly, half a pint of any nice green cooked vegetables cut up in little squares, such as French beans, artichoke bottoms, flageolets, peas, etc. Line the mould thinly with aspic jelly, then pour the mixture into it and leave it to set; when firm dip it into hot water, and turn it out on the dish. Any of the green purée left from the border can be mixed with some of the vegetables and mayonnaise for the centre.

FISH

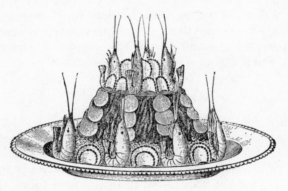

PRAWNS A LA PRINCESSE DE GALLES

Line a nest mould with aspic jelly about one eighth of an inch thick; cut out by means of a plain round cutter the purée of shrimps prepared as below in rounds about the size of a shilling piece, and arrange these up the side of the mould, allowing three rounds to each line; between these lines place little thin strips of French gherkin, some of which also place on the top of the mould; set this with aspic jelly, then fill up the centre with the mayonnaise mixture; when cold, dip the mould into hot water, pass a clean cloth over the bottom to absorb any moisture, then turn out on to a dish, and form a border with chopped aspic jelly; garnish round the border alternately with little thin rings of scalloped cucumber and large prawns (see engraving), arrange the top of the mould similarly, and serve for second course or for a cold collation, or in the fish course.

PURÉE OF SHRIMPS

Pound a quarter of a pound of picked shrimps with four boned anchovies, one large tablespoonful of thick béchamel sauce, one tablespoonful of salad oil, half a tablespoonful of tarragon vinegar, a little carmine, and a little coralline pepper; when pounded, pass through the hair sieve or tammy with a good half pint of aspic jelly, and put it into a sauté pan to get cold; then cut out as described above.

MIXTURE FOR CENTRE OF MOULD

Take three ounces of cooked lobster and a quarter of a pint of picked shrimps, and chop these together till fine; add a teaspoonful of chopped tarragon and chervil, or parsley, a dust of coralline pepper, eight or twelve small stoned and chopped olives, and two peeled tomatoes from which the pips have been removed; cut in dice shapes, mix all together with two tablespoonfuls of thick mayonnaise sauce and two and a half gills of liquid aspic jelly; continue stirring till the mixture begins to set, then use.

COD A LA GRAND HÔTEL

Cleanse the cod and cut it in slices about two inches thick, and sprinkle these well with salt. Let them stay in the salt for about an hour, then wash them well in cold water and tie them up with tape. Put about two ounces of butter, a dust of coralline pepper, the juice of a lemon, and about two and a half wineglasses of white wine (this is for three to four pounds of fish) in the bottom of a stewpan, lay the cod slices in this, with a buttered paper over them, and let it all simmer at the side of the stove for fifteen to twenty minutes, then take the fish up with a slice and place it on a hot dish, pour the sauce round it, with some more served in a sauceboat, and garnish the fillets all round the edge with salsify or parsnip cut in julienne shreds, and sprigs of picked and blanched chervil. Sprinkle the centre of the fish with a little lobster coral or coralline pepper. Serve very hot.

SALSIFY FOR GARNISH

Wash and peel the vegetables, cut them into shreds, and lay them in cold water and a little salt and lemon juice as you do them. Put them in a pan with enough boiling water seasoned with lemon juice and salt to cover them, bring the water to the boil, let them cook for an hour, then drain them, mix them with a little warm butter, coralline pepper, and use.

MAYONNAISE OF STUFFED TURBOT

Clean and wash a nice fresh turbot in cold salt and water, remove the fillets from the bone, place the underneath fillets together on a buttered tin, season with salt and coralline pepper, and then mask the inside of the fillets about a quarter of an inch thick with lobster farce as below, and on this lay the top fillets, pressing them as closely together as possible to present a natural appearance. Sprinkle the fish with strained lemon juice, place a buttered paper over it, and cook in a moderate oven, allowing twenty-five to thirty minutes for a fish large enough for fifteen to eighteen persons. When cooked put it aside to cool. Dish it when cold in the dish it is to be served in, mask it all over with very stiff mayonnaise sauce, smooth this with a wet palette knife and garnish with filleted anchovies, turned and farced olives, strips of French gherkins and of red chillies. Ornament the sides of the dish with prettily cut little blocks of aspic jelly and large prawns or slices of cooked lobster. This dish is excellent either for dinner or for a ball supper.

LOBSTER FARCE FOR TURBOT

Pound six ounces of cooked lobster till quite smooth, then mix to it three ounces of pounded panard, one tablespoonful of essence of anchovy, a dust of coralline pepper and a little carmine. Add two raw yolks of eggs and one raw white, rub all through a sieve, and use.

FILLETS OF SOLES WITH MUSHROOMS

Take out the fillets of two or three well-cleansed soles; free them of their black skin, season, and beat them slightly with the handle of a knife; pare, and mask them, on one side, with a thin layer of raw forcemeat; then fold them in two, on the masked side; place them in a flat stew-pan with melted butter, add the juice of two lemons, and fry them on both sides. Then drain, and pare them neatly, prick into each of them a crayfish claw (not peeled) in imitation of a ruffle or cuff; dish them on a border of fish force-meat, decorated, poached; fill its cavity with a garnish of white mushroom-buttons; mask the fillets and the garnish with some good velouté-sauce, reduced with extract of fish, and mushroom-trimmings; send up the remainder in a sauceboat.

FILLETS OF SALMON A LA BELLE ÎLE

Bat out some small fillets of salmon with a wet knife, spread on each a little of the farce given below, roll them up, tie a little band of buttered paper round each one, and cook them for fifteen minutes in the following marinade. Slice half a lemon and one small onion, and lay them with a bunch of herbs and four pepper-corns in a stewpan with a quarter of a pint of white wine and a gill of the stock in which the mussels required for this dish have been cooked (this quantity is enough for twelve small fillets). When the fillets are done remove the paper bands, lightly brush over the fillets with a little warm glaze, and serve them in little china or square paper cases (these latter must be well oiled out-side and then dried), and fill these up with the sauce given below, and garnish with quarters of cooked artichoke bottoms and prepared mussels. Serve these cases very hot, on a dish-paper or napkin. Two pounds of salmon is enough for twelve persons in this dish.

FARCE FOR FILLETS

Mix all together one teaspoonful of finely chopped truffle, four cooked (or tinned) artichoke bottoms cut up into tiny dice shapes, twelve mussels bearded and minced, and the fillets of four large smelts, freed from bone and chopped fine, with one ounce of fresh butter, the raw yolk of an egg, and a *very* little coralline pepper. Put into a forcing bag and arrange on the fillets.

MUSSELS FOR FILLETS

Allow two or three to each fillet. Soak them in cold water for an hour or so, then wash them well and put them in a stewpan with enough light stock to cover them, a glass of white wine, the bones of the filleted smelts, half a sliced onion, and six peppercorns. Bring this all to the boil, remove any scum, and allow it all to simmer gently for about five minutes, then take them up, remove the shells and the beards from the mussels and use. The beard of a mussel is the part that looks like seaweed.

SAUCE FOR FILLETS OF SALMON

When the salmon fillets are cooked, add to the liquor of the marinade sufficient of the stock in which the mussels were cooked to make the whole three quarters of a pint, and mix it on two ounces of butter and two ounces of flour which have been lightly fried but not discoloured, and stir all till it boils; add half a gill of cream and half an ounce of lobster spawn pounded, a dust of coralline pepper, let it all boil up again, stirring all the time, tammy and use. If the spawn is not obtainable, use a few drops of carmine.

CARP A LA MARINIERE

Draw a nice carp, weighing from six to eight pounds; scale it, shorten the fins, and fill the belly with forcemeat. Remove a little of the skin at each end, thus laying bare the flesh, and lard it with cut bacon. Truss the head of the carp, place it on the drainer of a fish-kettle; season it, and moisten to half its height with court-bouillon with wine nearly cold. Set the fish-kettle on the fire, to let the liquid boil; five minutes after, cover the carp with a thickly buttered paper, and push it into a moderate oven, to bake for an hour and a half, basting it often. Then take it out of the oven; drain it, to pass its stock through a sieve; put it back into a fish-kettle and keep it hot. With the cooking-stock prepare a little brown sauce; when clarified and strained, pour it into a flat stewpan, add a handful of trimmings of mushrooms; reduce it, introducing into it a glass of white wine, pass it through a sieve, and finish with four ounces of good butter.

Dish up the carp; surround it, on both sides, with a bunch of mushrooms, one of quenelles of whitings, and one of blanched olives; glaze the larding with a paste-brush, mask lightly the other parts of the fish, and the bottom of the dish, with a little sauce; and send up separately the remainder of the sauce, after having added to it the soft-roes.

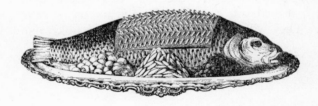

DEVILLED FISH

Take a teaspoonful of unmixed English mustard, a dessertspoonful of French mustard, ditto of chopped chutney, a dust of coralline pepper, a teaspoonful of essence of anchovy, four boned anchovies chopped fine, and a pinch of salt, and mix them together in a basin into a paste. Have the fish that is to be devilled steeped in a little warm butter, and then mask it over with the prepared paste, using a palette knife for the purpose; then sprinkle over it a few browned breadcrumbs, place a few pieces of butter here and there, and put it on a tin in the oven to cook for ten to fifteen minutes, according to the size of the fish. Dish up on a dish-paper; garnish with green parsley and coralline pepper. This is nice for fresh haddock or any remains of cold fish.

SCOLLOPED OYSTERS

Three dozen will make two scollops or one small dish. Take off the beards, boil the liquor with a blade of mace and a small piece of thin lemon peel, and strain it over the oysters; let them stand till cold. Take out the oysters, and season them with half a grain of cayenne, and half a saltspoonful of white pepper. Rub a thick slice of white bread, one day old, in a clean cloth till it is in very fine crumbs; mix with them the eighth part of a nutmeg, grated, half a saltspoonful of salt, and half a saltspoonful of white pepper. Lay the crumbs and the oysters in layers (either in two scollop-shells or a small tin dish), finishing with crumbs. Put half an ounce of butter in the centre of each shell, and half an ounce more on the top. Pour over each shell two dessertspoonfuls of the liquor, put them into a very quick oven, and bake to a pale golden colour. They will require about fifteen or eighteen minutes.

SLICE OF SALMON WITH MONTPELLIER BUTTER

Cut, off a large salmon, one slice three or four inches thick; cleanse, and place it in a stewpan, cover it with 'court-bouillon' half-cooled. Set the stewpan on the fire, bring the liquid to ebullition; then remove it back, cover the pan, and let the fish cool in its liquor. Then drain it carefully, dry it on a cloth, skin it, set it on a 'pain-vert', and mask it entirely with the 'montpellier butter', finished at the same time. Smooth its surface, equalising the more angular parts, place a small cooked lobster in the hollow of the 'darne'; decorate it by the aid of a cornet, filled with white butter, with cut-up gherkins, poached white of egg, fillets of anchovy, and whole capers; the decoration is according to fancy. Surround the 'darne' at its base with a string of chopped aspic-jelly, and the 'pain-vert' with fine croûtons of the same. Send up separately a boatful of mayonnaise sauce.

COURT-BOUILLON

Slice a large onion, one carrot, and a piece of celery-root; fry them in a stewpan with butter, oil or fat; moisten afterwards with either water and vinegar, or with white or red wine, mixed up with some hot water. Start the liquid to ebullition, remove it back, add to it salt, cloves, peppercorns, and a bunch of parsley and aromatics. Twenty minutes after, pass it through a sieve.

MONTPELLIER BUTTER

Put into a mortar the fillets of eight or ten salted anchovies; add a tablespoonful of chopped parsley, one of tarragon-leaves, one of burnet, and four of capers, also chopped up; pound the whole; add to the above five ounces of fresh butter, and pass it through a sieve. Place eight ounces of fresh butter in a warm kitchen-basin, work it with the spoon to render it frothy; then introduce into it the preparation, passed through a sieve; add a little green spinach-extract. Season, and make use of it immediately.

EEL WITH MONTPELLIER BUTTER

Take an eel well cleansed, remove its head and thin end; open it up the whole length, in order to remove the spine-bone, and to diminish the thickness of the meat; season, and fill it with a force-meat of fish, if desired to be lean; or if not, with a good 'galantine' forcemeat, prepared with the flesh of pike and fat bacon, in equal parts, pounded with a little panada.

The forcemeat being passed through a sieve, add a salpicon composed of truffles, fat liver, and pistachios. Sew the galantine, tie it up in a fine cloth, and boil it in a court-bouillon for two hours. Drain it afterwards, take it out of the cloth, wrap it up again; score, and roll it in a spiral way, forming it like a pyramid, in a stewpan, and round a dome-shaped mould. Let it cool entirely, take it out of the cloth, divest it of the thread, and put it on a decorated pain-vert having on its centre a support in the form of a dome. Adjust the head again (boiled separately) to the galantine, mask it with a thin coating of montpellier butter, ornament it with anchovy-butter squeezed through a cornet; surround its base with a thick string of jelly, and afterwards with a circle of hard-boiled eggs in quarters. Place around the pain-vert some bold croûtons of aspic-jelly, and serve separately a sauce-boatful of mayonnaise.

TO MAKE A FISH CURRY

Two spoonfuls of curry powder to half a pint of veal gravy; one or two large onions; a piece of butter the size of an egg; a spoonful of flour; any fish.

Mix two spoonfuls of curry powder with half a pint of veal gravy; one or two large onions; a piece of butter the size of an egg; a spoonful of flour. Whatever fish is used must be first fried, and then laid to drain and dry in a warm place. While it is doing, fry one or two large onions in butter, and when they are of a light brown colour, shake a spoonful of flour with them. When this is done, cut the fish carefully in pieces, put it on the onion, and strain the powder and gravy through a fine sieve on it, shake it a little, and let it boil for a quarter of an hour very slowly, close covered. When served, take up the fish with a slice or large knife and put it in a corner dish, then pour the sauce over it. Serve it with some tamarinds or lemons.

SKATE

Boil the skate with a tumblerful of milk, a little butter, two pinches of flour, two cloves, two shallots, a bayleaf, thyme, salt and pepper. Take him out of this, and strain the liquor. Put him next into a pie-dish, the bottom of which has been covered with grated Gruyère cheese. Intermix cunningly a dozen little onions, which have been already cooked. Surround the dish with fried crusts. Then pour upon the skate the strained sauce in which he has been cooked; cover him with more grated cheese, send him to the oven till he takes a fine colour, and rejoice over him.

MATELOTE

This is a stew of fresh-water fish. Take different kinds – carp, eel, pike, tench, perch – and cut them up; but it must be remembered that some of these fish, as the eel and the pike, may require some previous cooking to put them on the same level with the others. Put the pieces into a stewpan with two sliced onions, a faggot of sweet-herbs, two cloves of garlic crushed, two cloves, pepper and salt. Moisten all so as to be well-covered with a liquor composed of red wine two-thirds and broth one-third. Cook it on a brisk fire for twenty minutes; then pass the liquor through a tammy and keep the fish hot in the pan. In the meantime the relish or ragout of the fish will have been got ready as follows. Put half a pound of butter into a saucepan, and toss in it till they take a fine colour two dozen small onions; take out the onions, and put in their place two good spoonfuls of flour, which is to be worked into a roux. Add to this the strained liquor of the fish, the little onions, and a like quantity of mushrooms. Let the cooking go on till the onions and the mushrooms are sufficiently done; and then reduce the sauce on a quick fire and remove the grease from it. Lastly, make a pyramid of fish upon a dish, pour the sauce over it, and garnish it with crayfish and fried crusts of bread. The sauce thus prepared, with the garnish of onions, mushrooms, crayfish and crusts, is known as the Matelote Relish or Ragout.

EEL PIE

This used to be a famous pie, but we hear little of it now. The following is the Richmond receipt: Skin, cleanse and bone two Thames eels. Cut them in pieces and chop two small shallots. Pass the shallots in a little butter for five or six minutes, and then add to them a small faggot of parsley chopped, with nutmeg, pepper, salt, and two glasses of sherry. In the midst of this deposit the eels, add enough water to cover them, and set them on the fire to boil. When the boiling point is reached, take out the pieces of eel and arrange them in a pie-dish. In the meantime add to the sauce two ounces of butter kneaded with two ounces of flour, and let them incorporate by stirring over the fire. Finish the sauce with the juice of a whole lemon, and pour it among and over the pieces of eel in the pie-dish. Some slices of hard-boiled egg may be cunningly arranged on the top and in among the lower strata. Roof the whole with puff-paste; bake it for an hour and lo! a pie worthy of Eel-pie Island. It is a great question, debated for ages on Richmond Hill, whether this pie is best hot or cold. It is perfect either way.

COD'S HEAD AND SHOULDERS

The Scotch way, described by Meg Dods: 'This was a great affair in its day. It is still a formidable, nay, even a respectable-looking dish, with a kind of bulky magnificence, which, at Christmastide, appears imposing at the head of a long board. Have a quart of good stock made ready for the sauce, made of beef or veal, seasoned with onion, carrot and turnip. Rub the fish (a deep-sea or rock cod) with salt overnight, taking off the scales, but do not wash it. When to be dressed, wash it clean, then quickly dash hot water over the upper side, and with a blunt knife remove the slime which will ooze out, taking great care not to break the skin. Do the same to the other side of the fish; then place it on the drainer, wipe it clean, and plunge it into a fish-kettle of boiling water, with a handful of salt and a half-pint of vinegar. It must be entirely covered, and will take from thirty to forty minutes' slow boiling. Set it to drain, slide it carefully on a deep dish, and glaze with beaten eggs, over which strew fine breadcrumbs, grated lemon-peel, pepper and salt. Stick numerous bits of butter over the fish, and place it before a clear fire, strewing more crumbs, grated lemon-peel, and minced parsley over it, and basting with the butter. In the meanwhile thicken the stock with butter kneaded in flour, and strain it, adding to it half a hundred oysters nicely picked and bearded, and a glassful of their liquor, two glasses of Madeira or sherry, the juice of a lemon, the hard meat of a boiled lobster cut down, and the soft part pounded. Simmer this sauce for five minutes, and skim it well; wipe clean the edges of the dish in which the fish is crisping, and pour the half of the sauce around it, serving the rest in a tureen.' It will be found, however, that French white wine is better for a fish sauce than sherry or Madeira. And the lobster added to the oysters is a superfluity.

MEAT

HOT POT OF MUTTON

Take some neck or loin of mutton for this dish and cut it in cutlets, allowing one to each person; remove all unnecessary fat and skin from them, season well with coralline pepper and salt, and place on each cutlet or chop three or four slices of raw mutton kidney, arrange them neatly in a greased pie-dish so that they slightly overlap each other, sprinkle them with finely chopped shallot and chopped parsley, and place one or two bearded oysters on the top of the kidney. Have some blanched potatoes cut in rounds about a quarter of an inch thick, stamp them out with a plain round cutter about two inches in diameter, then arrange these in coils all over the cutlets; pour into the dish the liquor from the oysters and half a pint of good gravy; break up in small pieces one ounce of butter and sprinkle on the potatoes, place a buttered paper over and stand the dish in a tin with a little boiling water underneath it; let it remain in the oven for about two hours, occasionally adding a little more gravy, then dish it on a dish-paper or napkin. Sprinkle a little finely chopped parsley and a few French capers and coralline pepper over the top, and serve very hot. This is a nice dish for a *relevé* for luncheon, and also for sending out for shooting parties, and can be used instead of a joint for a small party. Game and poultry would also be good cooked in the same way, the birds, of course, being first boned and then cut up.

CHÂTEAUBRIANI STEAK AND FRIED POTATOES

Cut the fillet of beef one and a half to two inches thick; trim off all unnecessary fat and skin; season with salt, coralline pepper, and salad oil, and let it lie in the seasoning for at least one hour before cooking; then put it on oiled straws, between two thin slices from the neck of beef, which can afterwards be used up in other ways, and cook for twelve to fifteen minutes over a bright fire; then dish up, and serve with fried potatoes and a sauce prepared thus: Put a wineglassful of white wine into a stewpan; then mix into it one ounce of glaze, four good tablespoonfuls of brown sauce, and a few drops of carmine; boil up together, and add by degrees two ounces of fresh butter, working it in bit by bit; when the butter has dissolved mix in a teaspoonful of chopped parsley and half the juice of a lemon, and a tiny pinch of castor sugar; pour over the fillet, and serve at once. The fillet is best when grilled.

FRIED OX EARS

Take the ox ears, scald them, remove all the hair by means of a small knife, then wash them well in several waters, and when perfectly clean put them into a stewpan with enough cold water to cover, and a little salt. When it comes to the boil, strain and rinse in cold water, and then put them into some stock or water and flavour well with vegetables, such as carrot, onion, celery, leek, and herbs such as thyme, parsley, bayleaf, basil, marjoram, and twelve to fifteen peppercorns; boil gently for eight to ten hours, then take up and put to press between two plates till cold; then cut each ear into three or four pieces, and steep in warm butter, season with a little fresh chopped mushroom that has been washed, a little chopped shallot, parsley, thyme, bayleaf, and mignonette pepper, and dip into whole beaten-up egg and into freshly made white breadcrumbs, and fry in clean boiling fat until a pretty golden colour. Dish up on a paper and garnish with fried potatoes or parsley, and serve piquant sauce in a boat. This is a nice dish for an entrée for dinner or luncheon. Pigs' and calves' ears done in a similar manner are nice.

PIQUANT SAUCE

Chop up one shallot, and put it into a stewpan with two bayleaves, a sprig of thyme, a pinch of mignonette pepper, and four table-spoonfuls of French vinegar; reduce to half the quantity, then mix with three quarters of a pint of brown sauce, one ounce of glaze, or a teaspoonful of extract of meat, and a pinch of sugar; boil together for about ten minutes, then wring through the tammy, and mix with a dessertspoonful of chopped capers, two or three chopped French gherkins, a few drops of carmine, a dust of coral-line pepper, and a pinch of chopped parsley; boil up, then use.

SHEEP'S EARS IN CROUSTADE

Scald a dozen sheep's ears; singe, and boil them; when drained and cold, fill them inwardly with a layer of raw forcemeat, thus supporting them in an upright position; dip them into beaten eggs, bread-crumb, and fry them.

On the other hand, prepare a pound and a quarter of potato purée; as soon as passed through a sieve, season; introduce into it a piece of butter, a handful of grated Parmesan, and ten yolks of eggs; pour it on a floured table, and work with the hand, gradually introducing flour enough to render firm; place it then on a round of paper, cut-up of the size of a round dish. With this composition, prepare a croustade of low form, making the flutings with a piece of carrot cut slantwise, and leaving a hollow in the centre of the cut. When done, egg, and push it into a hot oven, to take colour. Then take it up, slip it on a dish, fill the hollow with minced mushrooms, and thereon place the ears upright. Glaze them, and send apart a brown sauce, reduced with trimmings of mushrooms.

PIGS' FEET A LA CENDRILLON

Blanch four pigs' feet by putting them in cold water with a pinch of salt and bringing them to the boil, and then put them to cook until tender; take out the bones and fill the feet with farce; arrange them with sliced truffle on the top and wrap them in cleansed pork caul; then brush them over with white of egg and sprinkle browned breadcrumbs all over, with the exception of that part which is decorated with the truffle; cook in the oven on a buttered tin for fifteen minutes. Dish on a purée of mushrooms with the sauce round the base.

SAUCE FOR PETITS PIEDS A LA CENDRILLON

To half a pint of brown sauce add a wineglassful of white wine, a good teaspoonful of French mustard, a dust of coralline pepper, and a saltspoonful of English mustard; boil up, tammy, and use.

FARCE FOR PETITS PIEDS A LA CENDRILLON

Pound half a pound of loin of pork and pass it through the machine, then mix with it a saltspoonful of mignonette pepper, a dust of coralline pepper, a pinch of salt, three chopped truffles or mushrooms, one eschalot chopped fine, and one raw yolk of egg; mix all together and put into a forcing bag with a pipe and use.

LARDED FILLET OF BEEF A LA TROUVILLE

Take three or four pounds of fillet of beef and trim off all the unnecessary fat and skin from it, lard it with fat bacon, cut into lardons about two inches long, putting three or four lines of lardons according to the size of the fillet; trim the lardons and tie up the fillet in three or four places; put two ounces of butter on the bottom of a stewpan with one large sliced carrot, two sliced onions, a few pieces of celery cut up, a cut up turnip, a bunch of herbs, thyme, parsley, bayleaf, and about ten black and white peppercorns; put the fillet of beef on these and fry it for about twenty minutes, then add about a quarter of a pint of stock and put the pan into the oven, braise the fillet for about two and a half hours, keeping it constantly basted over the paper and adding more stock as that in the pan reduces. When cooked, take out the fillet, remove the strings, brush it over with glaze and put it again in the oven for about ten minutes to crisp; dish up the fillet on a dish on some spaghetti prepared as below, and hâtelet skewers can also be arranged in the fillet if liked. Strain the gravy from the braise, remove all the fat, put the gravy into a stewpan with about half a pint of brown sauce, a wineglass of sherry, half an ounce of glaze, and a pinch of sugar; let it reduce a quarter part, keeping it skimmed while boiling, pass it through a tammy, add a few drops of carmine and a good dust of coralline pepper; just boil it up and serve in a sauceboat.

SPAGHETTI FOR GARNISH

Put a quarter of a pound of spaghetti in a stewpan with enough boiling water to cover it, season it with a little salt, simmer it for about thirty minutes, then strain it and mix with a quarter of a pound of grated Parmesan cheese, a good dusting of coralline pepper, a pinch of salt, and four tablespoonfuls of tomato butter; reboil all together and use.

BEARS' PAWS RUSS FASHION

In Russia bears' paws are sold ready-skinned, as commonly, perhaps, as pigs' feet elsewhere. Although this is a dish little known in Central Europe, it may yet be appetising for the people of the West.

Wash the bears' paws, wipe, salt, and put them into a kitchen-basin; cover them with cooked marinade, and thus let them macerate for two or three days.

Spread a stewpan with trimmings of bacon and ham, and sliced vegetables; place the paws thereupon, moisten (covered) with their marinade and the broth, half-and-half; cover them with thin layers of bacon, and boil them for seven or eight hours on a slow fire, adding more broth as the stock reduces.

The paws being tender, leave them in their stock till nearly cold; drain, wipe, and divide each of them in four pieces lengthwise; sprinkle over cayenne pepper, roll them in melted lard, bread-crumb, and broil them for half an hour on a very slow fire; then dish up. Pour on the bottom of the dish some piquant sauce finished with two tablespoonfuls of red-currant jelly.

SHOULDERS OF LAMB, IN DUCK-LIKE FORM

Get three shoulders of lamb, leaving part of the leg adhering; bone them without removing the thin-end bone, and season inwardly.

Prepare some quenelle forcemeat with some lamb or veal meat, in the same proportions as for veal quenelle; when passed through a sieve, add half its volume of salpicon, composed of cooked ham, lamb-sweetbreads, and mushrooms. With this preparation stuff the shoulders, sew them to an oblong form, truss with the thin-end bone upright, shaping them to the shape of a duck: the shoulder of lamb lending itself by nature to the imitation. Place them afterwards in a stewpan, in the same way they are to be served; moisten to cover with tepid water, warm until the skin be set; then drain the shoulders, steep them in cold water, wipe, and lard, on both sides, the part standing for the body of the duck.

The meats being larded, surround the neck, or rather the thin-end bone of the shoulders, with layers of bacon, put them into the bottom of a stewpan, prepared as for braise, support them with large vegetables, and moisten to height with good broth. Let them boil quickly for ten minutes, then remove the pan back; cover them with buttered paper, and finish braising them with hot ashes on the lid, basting frequently.

At last, glaze them to a nice colour; drain them, remove the string, and cut them slightly underneath, thus giving them the required 'aplomb'. Pare the top of the bone, imitate the eyes with a round of tongue, or ham; dish up, and surround with a garnish of mushrooms and olive. Dilute their stock with a little wine; let it boil, strain, skim off the fat, add to it the liquor of the mushrooms, and reduce to half; thicken it then with a little brown sauce. With this sauce, mask the bottom of the dish, and send the surplus in a sauceboat.

KIDNEY STEWED WITH CHAMPAGNE

A veal kidney, or some sheep's kidneys; two ounces of butter; one onion; a quarter of a pint of Champagne; a spoonful of mushroom ketchup; a spoonful of stock or gravy; pepper and salt.

Take a veal kidney or some sheep's kidneys, cut them in thin slices with a sharp knife, fry them in butter a nice brown, with an onion cut very thin. Then put them into a stewpan (free from the butter) with a quarter of a pint of Champagne or white wine, a little mushroom ketchup, a spoonful of stock or gravy, and some pepper and salt. Stew gently until tender and then serve very hot.

TO MAKE SAUSAGES OF PORK

Such proportions of pork, fat and lean mixed, as you please; to every ten pounds of meat put four ounces of fine salt and one ounce of fine pepper; one teaspoonful of dried sage or lemon thyme; one teaspoonful of ground allspice and cloves.

Chop the meat as fine as possible, and mix the seasoning well through the whole. Have ready some hog's intestines to put the sausage meat into. They are thus prepared: Empty them; cut them in lengths and lay them for three or four days in salt and water, or weak lime-water; turn them inside out once or twice; scrape them; then rinse them, and they are ready to fill with meat, which is put into them, and the ends left empty to tie over. If you prefer using the sausage meat without this case, then you must make it up the size and shape of sausages, dip each in beaten egg, and then in wheat flour, and fry them in hot lard. Turn them over and over in the pan to brown them nicely. Serve them (drained from the fat) on toasted bread. They are also used as garnishing for turkey. Or you may form the sausage meat into round cakes, fry as above, and serve them round a mould of mashed potatoes when you have roast fowl for dinner. By increasing the quantity of sausage meat in these proportions, you will have enough to keep for future use. Put it into stone jars, packing it closely, and covering it tightly down.

MINCED MUTTON

One pound and a half of meat, half a pint of good brown gravy; pepper and salt; six or seven eggs.

Take a pound and a half of dressed mutton, and mince it as fine as possible, season it highly with salt and pepper, warm half a pint of good brown gravy, or gravy made from the bones, make the mince very hot in it, and send it to the table with a border of poached eggs.

BEEF GOBBETS

Some slices of beef; a little mace; three cloves; some whole peppers; half a stick of celery; two turnips; two carrots; a sprig of parsley; a bunch of sweet herbs; one ounce of rice; one slice of bread; one French roll.

Take any part of beef except the leg, cut into small pieces, and put them into a stewpan, cover them with water, and when they have stewed for an hour put in a *very* little mace, three cloves, and some whole peppers tied in a piece of muslin, with half a head of celery cut very small; then add some salt, the carrots and turnips cut in slices, the sprigs of parsley and herbs, a large *crust* of bread, and an ounce of rice; cover it close and let it stew until tender, then take out the herbs, spices, and bread. Have ready a French roll toasted and cut into four parts, put these into your dish, put in the meat, pour the sauce over it and serve very hot.

OX-CHEEK CHEESE –
A HOMELY AMERICAN RECEIPT

Half an ox-head; one teaspoonful of fine salt; half a teaspoonful of pepper; one tablespoonful of powdered thyme; enough water to cover the head.

Split an ox-head in two, take out the eyes, crack the side bones, and lay it in water for one whole night. Then put it in a saucepan with sufficient water to cover it. Let it boil very gently, skimming it carefully. When the meat loosens from the bones take it from the water with a skimmer, and put it into a bowl. Take out every particle of bone, chop the meat very fine, and season it with a teaspoonful of salt, and half a teaspoonful of pepper; add a table-spoonful of powdered thyme. Tie it in a cloth and press it with a weight. When cold it may be cut in slices for dinner or supper. The gravy remaining will make a rich broth if a few vegetables be stewed in it.

OX-TONGUES A LA FINANCIÈRE

Get two fine ox-tongues, either fresh or pickled; if fresh, blanch them and then braise; if the tongues are salted, they must be simply boiled, in plenty of water, on a mild fire. At serving-time, drain both the tongues, round them neatly on their thickest part, and from this part cut off one piece, which then carve into regular slices. Dish the two tongues, in the order represented by the drawing, but applying them against a support of fried bread fixed on the dish, then masked with some raw forcemeat, which is poached in the oven. Bring back into its place the piece cut off, entirely glaze the tongues, surround them on their basis with a 'ragoût à la financière', surround the ragout with a garnish of quenelles formed with the spoon, and other quenelles studded with truffles; send up separately a boatful of good brown sauce, reduced with a little Madeira.

TO BOIL REINDEER TONGUES

The proper way to prepare reindeer tongues for boiling, is to soak them in a pan of water for three hours, and then expose them to the air; this must be repeated three times. Then scrape them very clean, put them into a stewpan of cold water, and bring them gradually to boil. Let them simmer slowly, skimming them carefully all the time. Serve them on a table napkin.

A TURTLE BOTTOM DISH

Three bottles of Madeira; four quarts of strong veal gravy; one lemon; a bunch of sweet herbs; six anchovies; a teaspoonful of

3—TVCB * *

cayenne pepper; four ounces of beaten mace; a teaspoonful of mushroom powder; half a pint of essence of ham.

Cut off the head of the turtle, and take care of the blood. Take off the fins, and lay them in salt and water. Cut off the bottom shell, and cut off the meat which grows to it – this is the calipee, or fowl, of cookery books. Take out the heart, liver and lights, and lay them by themselves. Take out the bones, and the flesh out of the back shell, which is the calipash of cookery books. Cut the fleshy part into pieces about two inches square, but leave the fat part which looks green; it is called the monsieur; rub it with salt, then wash it in several waters to make it thoroughly clean. Put in the pieces that you took out, with three bottles of Madeira, four quarts of strong veal gravy, a lemon cut in slices, a bunch of sweet herbs (sweet basil must be one of them), six anchovies washed and picked clean, a teaspoonful of cayenne pepper, four ounces of beaten mace, a teaspoonful of mushroom powder, and half a pint of essence of ham, if you have it. Lay over it a coarse paste, and set it in the oven for three hours. When it comes out skim off the fat, and brown the top with a salamander.

BOILED HAM

Soak an English ham for twenty-four, a Spanish one for forty-eight hours. Scrape it and cleanse it carefully. Boil it or braise it in liquor and seasoning enough to cover it. For very simple tastes water alone is used, together with carrots, onions, celery, cloves, mace, thyme and bayleaves. For a very fine ham use a mirepoix into which about a pint of wine enters, and add broth to make up the remainder of the liquor. For something between these two take a quart of cider, together with carrots, onions, and a faggot of sweet-herbs, using water for whatever else of liquor may be required. Simmer it or braise it very slowly indeed for four or five hours, according to size. Then lift it out of its pan – take off the rind and let it dry for a minute or two in the oven – after which it is to be trimmed, and it may be either glazed in the French fashion, or in English fashion strewed with raspings. If the ham is to be served cold let it cool in its liquor, then remove the rind, trim it, cover it either with glaze or with raspings, and garnish it with aspic jelly and picked parsley.

CALF'S HEAD

Plain boiled – the English way. Take a whole or half a head. Scald it well, and let it soak for an hour or two in cold water. Then simmer it for an hour and a half in water enough to make it swim, and with a faggot of pot-herbs. Serve it with maître d'hôtel sauce (parsley and butter) poured over it; and let it be garnished with bacon or pig's cheek, with the tongue nicely trimmed, and with the brains which have been cooked apart.

The French way. The head or half-head is first boned, then blanched as above, then cut in pieces, keeping the ear apart with a good base to it, then simmered for an hour and a half with the faggot of pot-herbs. The pieces of calf's head are next drained, the tongue is trimmed, and all are served in naked simplicity on an oval dish; the ear-pieces, which are considered the tit-bits, being made conspicuous in the arrangement. It is eaten either hot or cold with a cruet sauce. As many people like to make this sauce in proportions selected by themselves, it is usual to serve with it, on a plate and in separate heaps, capers, chives and parsley – the last two chopped.

CALF'S HEAD A LA FINANCIÈRE

Blanch a nice boned calf's head; when refreshed and singed cut its ears round, and divide the remainder of the head into pieces of equal size; place the ears upright in a stewpan, with the pieces of head surrounding them, moisten with a sufficient quantity of very fat and white broth, and some wine; cover with a buttered paper, and boil them on a slow fire. Boil separately two nice calves' brains.

On the other hand, cut a fluted bread-croustade of an oval form, make a circular incision on its top, and fry it to a nice colour; empty it afterwards, and mask it on the top, with a layer of raw forcemeat; fix it (by the aid of small skewers) on a stand of fried bread, stuck on the centre of an oblong dish, and keep it at the entrance of the oven. When time to serve, drain the ears, and other pieces of calf's head; pare away the fat, only preserving the skinny parts, which cut with a plain round cutter. Pare the ears, hollow them with a cutter, score the auricle, then place them upright at each end of the dish, on a layer of poached forcemeat.

Drain the brains, dish them on each side of the croustade occupying the centre of the dish; garnish the hollow, between the ears and the brains, on one side with a group of small quenelles moulded with the spoon, and on the other with a group of button-mushrooms.

Fill the cavity of the croustade with quenelles and mushrooms; range round the pieces of head in a close circle, and garnish the centre with truffles and cocks' combs. Mask slightly the garnishes, and the bottom of the dish, with a little Madeira sauce; the remainder of which pour into a sauceboat. Insert on the top of the croustade, on each side, a hâtelet-skewer, garnished with truffles of different sizes.

LITTLE BOMBES OF VEAL A LA GELÉE

Take some little bombe moulds and line them thinly with liquid aspic jelly, garnish the tops with finely shredded lettuce and little strips of truffle and red chilli; arrange round the moulds little sprigs of chervil, and set all the garnish with aspic jelly. Then line the moulds again with aspic cream, and when this is set fill up the moulds with a cream of veal prepared as below, put them aside until firm, then dip each into hot water, and turn out the bombes on to a cloth, arrange them on an entrée dish as shown in the engraving, place a wax figure in the centre, and garnish with cooked vegetables or a salad, seasoned with a little salad oil, tarragon and chilli vinegar, and a little finely chopped shallot. Use for an entrée for dinner or luncheon, or for ball supper, etc.

CREAM OF VEAL

Take half a pound of cooked veal, two tablespoons of velouté sauce, a wineglassful of sherry, and a pinch of salt; pound till smooth, then add to it half a pint of liquid aspic jelly in which four sheets of gelatine have been dissolved; rub through a fine hair sieve, then mix with half a gill of stiffly whipped cream, and pour into the moulds when beginning to set.

VELOUTÉ SAUCE

One and a half ounces of fine flour, one and a half ounces of butter; mix well together, and let it fry gently on the side of the stove till a very pale colour; then mix it with three-quarters of a pint of nicely flavoured stock, either veal, rabbit, or chicken. Stir till it boils; add a quarter of a pint of cream, a pinch of salt, and three or four drops of lemon juice; keep boiling for about five minutes; keep skimmed, tammy, and use. The thick creamy velouté sauce may be made by reducing this a quarter part.

LITTLE CREAMS OF HAM ICED

Whip half a pint of cream until quite stiff, then mix it with a quarter of a pint of liquid aspic jelly and a few drops of carmine to make it a pale salmon colour, add a dust of coralline pepper, and five ounces of lean cooked ham that is cut up in very little dice shapes; stir all together over ice until it begins to set, then put it in a Neapolitan ice mould and place this in the ice cave for about one and a half hours; when sufficiently iced dip the mould in cold water, remove the covers, and turn the ham cream on to a clean cloth, cut it in slices crossways, and dish them up on a dish-paper in a round, overlapping one another; garnish the centre with a bunch of picked mustard and cress or any nice salad, and decorate the slices with ham butter by means of bag and fancy pipe.

TURBAN OF RABBIT A LA PLUCHE

Take a cleansed and skinned rabbit, remove the back fillets and cut them into as many nice fillets as possible, bat them out with a cold wet chopping knife; lard the top part of the fillets with some very finely cut lardons of bacon, and trim the lardons neatly and evenly. Well butter and paper a turban mould and fill it up by means of a bag and pipe with the farce prepared as below; place it in a stewpan on a fold of paper, surround it with boiling water to three parts of its depth, place the pan on the stove and watch the water re-boil, then draw it aside and poach the turban until firm; when cooked turn it out of the mould on to a paste bottom, and when cold mask it over with plain white farce, arrange the larded fillets all over this as shown in the engraving, fixing them to the turban with more farce, garnish between each fillet with little bunches of French gherkin, truffle, and cooked bacon or lean ham, using a little farce to keep them in place, fill up the centre of the turban with a band of well-buttered paper and surround the outside similarly; place it on a baking-tin, brush it over with warm butter, cook it in a rather quick oven for thirty-five to forty minutes, and when getting a nice brown colour brush it over with warm glaze, and sprinkle it with grated Parmesan cheese; replace it in the oven to crisp, and if the oven is not sufficiently quick, brown the fillets with a hot salamander; take up the turban, remove the papers, and place it on a hot entrée dish, pour the sauce (prepared as below) round, and arrange in the centre by means of a bag and large rose pipe, a purée of chestnuts or spinach, with a hâtelet skewer in the centre. Serve for a hot entrée for a dinner party.

FARCE FOR TURBAN

Take half a pound of raw rabbit, or white meat, free it from bone, and cut it up; also take a quarter of a pound of panard, a quarter of a pound of cooked ham, one ounce of finely chopped blanched beef marrow or suet, one finely chopped shallot, a teaspoonful of chopped parsley, half an ounce of grated Parmesan, a little salt, and coralline pepper; pound the meat, then pound the panard, mix it with a tablespoonful of thick cream and three whole raw eggs; rub the purée through a fine wire sieve, add to it the marrow and other ingredients, colour with a few drops of carmine, mix up together, and use as instructed.

SAUCE FOR TURBAN

Take one pint of good velouté sauce, and when it is boiling add to it one ounce of grated Parmesan cheese, stir till re-boiling, then mix into the sauce a quarter of a pint of thick cream, in which three raw yolks of egg and the juice of a lemon have been mixed, a teaspoonful of French mustard, and the same of English mustard; stir again on the fire till thickening, but do not allow it to boil; then tammy and use.

PASTE BOTTOM

Rub one ounce of butter into a quarter of a pound of flour till smooth, and add to it half a raw egg, and mix with cold water into a very stiff paste, roll out about a quarter of an inch thick, cut the paste in a round shape to fit the turban mould, place it on a buttered tin and prick the paste well, and bake in a moderate oven for about half an hour, and use.

LAMB CUTLETS A LA RICHMOND

Take the best end of the neck of lamb and have it neatly trimmed and cut into small cutlets; season with coralline pepper and salt and place them in a buttered sauté pan and lightly sauté, then put to press; when they are cold, thinly mask over with the beef farce prepared as below; smooth this over with a warm knife (made so by dipping the knife in boiling water), egg, and breadcrumbs. Press them neatly into shape with the palette knife and ornament with cut truffle. Place them in a sauté pan with two or three table-spoonfuls of boiling clarified butter and fry till a nice golden colour. Dish on a border of potato and serve artichoke bottoms in the centre which have been blanched and cooked in water with a little salt and a little lemon juice, strained and cut in four or five pieces, according to size, and seasoned with a few drops of lemon juice, a tablespoonful of thick cream and a very little chopped tarragon and chervil. Serve tomato butter round the base. The cutlets should be served very hot. Cut the truffle for garnishing the cutlets in the shape of a kite, and use eight pieces to each cutlet with a small round of the same in the centre. Make a farce in the usual manner with six ounces of scraped raw beef, three ounces of panard, half an ounce of butter, a little pepper and salt, and one and a half raw eggs; pass through a fine wire or hair sieve; mix into the farce a dessertspoonful of chopped truffle and tongue or ham, then use.

EPIGRAMS OF MUTTON A LA REITZ

Remove all unnecessary fat from the thin end of a breast of mutton, tie it up with string, and braise it for two and a half hours, then take up the breast, remove the bones, season with chopped parsley, shallot, coralline pepper and salt, and put it to press between two dishes and when cold stamp it out in the shape of cutlets with a cutlet cutter; strain and take off the fat from the gravy of the braise, lay half of the cutlets in this, and let them just come to the boil and remain so for ten minutes; flour, egg and breadcrumb the other pieces, and fry them in clean boiling fat for about eight minutes, then sprinkle the plain pieces with gherkin, tongue, truffle, mushroom and cooked celery all cut into julienne shreds. Dish up *en couronne*, alternating the pieces, and serve a purée of mushrooms or vegetables in the centre. Réforme sauce round. The trimmings can be used for a shepherd's pie or mutton broth.

RÉFORME SAUCE

One ounce of glaze, one wineglassful of claret or port, three quarters of a pint of brown sauce, the juice of one lemon, pinch of castor sugar, a few drops of carmine, a dust of coralline pepper, and one large tablespoonful of red currant jelly; boil and keep skimmed till reduced a quarter part, then tammy and use.

LITTLE TONGUES A LA PRINCESSE MARIE

Take three quarters of a pound of raw rabbit, veal, or chicken, half a pound of fresh fat and lean pork or ham, a quarter of a pound of pounded panard, and one large tablespoonful of thick brown sauce; pound these and rub the purée through a fine wire sieve, then mix it in a basin with three raw yolks of eggs, a pinch of salt and coralline pepper, add to it two ounces of chopped lean ham or tongue, and two truffles chopped fine. Butter some tongue moulds and fill them by means of a bag and pipe with the prepared mixture, place them in a saucepan, sprinkle with a little sherry, put a buttered paper over, and cook in a moderate oven for fifteen minutes, keeping them well basted; when cooked take up the tongues and put them aside till cold, then turn them out of the moulds and mask them with fawn-coloured chaudfroid sauce and aspic cream, after which glaze them over with liquid aspic jelly and dish on a border prepared as below with a block of rice in the centre; garnish with a purée of peas, and serve for a cold entrée or for a cold collation.

CHAUDFROID (BROWN) SAUCE

Three quarters of a pint of aspic, quarter of a pint of tomato sauce, a few drops of carmine, half a wineglassful of sherry, half an ounce of glaze and a dust of coralline pepper; reduce a quarter part, keep skimmed while boiling, then tammy and use when somewhat cool.

BORDER FOR TONGUES

Take a pint of cooked peas, drain them from the water, rub them through a wire sieve, and mix with the purée three raw eggs, one ounce of warm butter, a little salt and white pepper, and a dust of chopped mint; mix up together, then put it into a buttered border mould which has been garnished all over with cooked whole peas, and stand it in a tin containing boiling water to about three fourths its depth; put a buttered paper over, place the tin in a moderate oven, and poach till firm, which will take about twenty minutes. Put the mould aside until cool, then dip it into hot water, turn out the border, and use. This border would also be nice to serve with hot entrées.

TIMBALE, SNAIL-LIKE FASHION

Butter the inside of a dome-mould. Take a pound and a quarter of fine short paste, divide it into several parts, which roll into strings, the size of macaroni; place them against the sides of the mould, beginning at the centre, then spread over the paste a layer of fresh pork mince, mixed up with a chopped truffle. Cut into scollops, two or three scalded sweetbreads, cooled under weight. Fry, in melted fat-bacon, a few spoonfuls of fine-herbs; onions, shallot, mushrooms; when their moisture is evaporated, add six ounces of raw ham, in small dice, and the scollops of sweetbreads, toss them over a brisk fire for a few minutes, and season. When the sweetbreads are well set, pour over three tablespoonfuls of Madeira;

after a few seconds, take them off the fire, and sprinkle over some chopped parsley.

The ragout being about cold, arrange it by layers in the timbale, alternated with some calf's brains, blanched, and cut up like the sweetbreads. Cover the timbale with a flat of paste, which solder carefully; place the mould on a layer of ashes, put it on a baking-sheet and bake it in a moderate oven for one hour.

When done, take it from the fire, make a small hole in the cover, through which pour into the timbale a few spoonfuls of brown sauce, reduced, but not too thick; turn it out on its dish, and set a button-mushroom on the top.

POULTRY & GAME

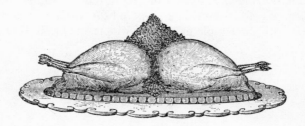

ROAST PHEASANTS WITH CRESS

Let the birds be hung by the under part of the beak separately on hooks, and sufficiently long to develop their flavour; for this purpose a cold, dry, and above all a thoroughly airy place should be chosen. About four days' hanging in such a place will generally meet the requirements; but when a 'higher' state is wished for let the birds hang until the feathers from the under part at the tail end are easily detached. When the bird has reached the required degree of flavour pluck it, remove the crop by making an incision in the back of the neck, taking care not to break the skin of the crop, and remove the entrails by cutting the vent slightly, singe and truss it for roasting, but in no case wash it; tie a piece of fat slitted bacon over the breast and roast it for fifteen to twenty minutes in front of a quick fire, the exact time, of course, depending on whether the bird has to be well done or underdone. It is an essential point, and one that cannot be too strongly insisted upon, that the bird must be well basted during the roasting, especially during the beginning, for if it once becomes dry in any part, no amount of after attention can rectify it. If proper convenience is not at hand for roasting, baking can be resorted to; but the necessity for basting would be even more urgent. When the bird is cooked it should be immediately transferred to a piece of trimmed and buttered toast or a croûton, which may be in one piece, or cut into three or four, according to whether the bird is to be served whole to each person or carved. When placed on the toast on a dish, garnish it with watercress and hand with it browned breadcrumbs, bread sauce, and gravy prepared from game bones; and in no case should the gravy be sent to table on the same dish as the bird. The slitted bacon may or may not be served with the bird. Such is the proper service when served hot, either for breakfast, luncheon or second course dinner dish; but when served cold it should be prepared the same way, and sent to the table with the simple garnish of watercress or fresh parsley.

SMALL COLD PATTIES OF LARKS

Bone seven larks, reserving their heads; season, stuff them with a stuffing prepared as follows: Slice four ounces of calves' liver, fry it with lard, add to it the trails of the larks, a pinch of chopped onion, a few sprigs of aromatics, and some trimmings of truffles, seasoning the whole well; the liver and trails being done, take them off the fire, allow to cool, and pound them with half their volume of chopped fresh bacon; then add two or three truffles in small dice. With this stuff the larks. Shape them round, surround them with a strip of buttered paper, and braise them short of moisture; let them cool, then pare, glaze them with a paste-brush, and mask them with a thin coating of aspic jelly.

On the other hand, bake twelve small channelled pie-crusts; when cold, mask them at the bottom, and all round, with a preparation of purée of cooked livers, diluted with a little chaufroid sauce; half-fill the crusts with chopped aspic, and set the galantines thereon. Insert on the top of each a lark's head, previously cooked, and glazed with a paste-brush. Dish the small patties then on a folded napkin.

TURKEY, BOILED, A L'ÉCARLATE

Singe a turkey, draw, fill it with stuffing of breadcrumbs and beef suet (chopped), so as to get it quite round; truss the turkey, as for boiling, and place it in an oblong stewpan with aromatics, pepper-corns, cloves, and a few sprigs of fresh celery leaves.

Two hours previous to serving, moisten the turkey, to its height, with hot broth and toppings; set the stewpan on the fire; let the liquid boil up, cover the turkey with a buttered paper, and boil it for two hours, covered, and on a moderate fire, that the cooking-stock may not be reduced too much.

On the other hand, boil two pickled ox-tongues, being careful to put them on the fire soon enough to be done at the same time with the turkey, and keep them in their stock till ready to serve. When the turkey is done, strain the cooking-stock, and skim off the fat, which pour over the turkey.

With a pint of turkey cooking-stock prepare a little white sauce, stir the sauce on the fire, to thicken; as soon as boiling, take it off, thicken with three yolks of eggs, boil without allowing it to boil up, and pass it through a sieve.

When ready to serve, drain turkey and tongues, remove the string from the turkey, and set it on an oblong dish; make a decoration on the breast with tarragon-leaves, and surround it, at its base, with slices of tongue cut off the thickest parts; pour on the bottom of the dish a little good gravy, and pour the sauce into a sauceboat.

The dish itself is placed on a hot-water-dish.

POULARDE A LA VALENCIENNE

Prepare a poularde for braising and lard the breast with lardons of fat bacon, put it into a stewpan with two ounces of butter, two sliced onions, one sliced carrot, a large bunch of herbs, six or eight peppercorns, and four or five cloves; place the poularde on the vegetables, cover it with a well-buttered paper, fry for fifteen to twenty minutes, then add to it about half a pint of stock and put into a moderate oven, and braise it with the pan covered down for about three quarters of an hour, adding more stock as that in the pan reduces, and keeping the fowl well basted. When cooked take it up and remove the string or trussing skewers, then place it on a baking tin, and brush over with a little warm glaze; replace in the oven for about ten minutes to crisp the lardons and dish up on the rice prepared as below; strain the gravy, remove the fat from it, and serve in a sauceboat with the poularde, and should there not be sufficient gravy left from the braise, add a little more good hot stock to it before straining.

Prepare the rice for dishing the fowl up on by putting three quarters of a pound of Patna rice into a stewpan to blanch, then wash it and put it back into the saucepan with half a pint of tomato pulp and half a pint of stock that has been coloured with a little carmine, add a bunch of herbs, two ounces of butter, a quarter of an ounce of coralline pepper; watch the rice coming to the boil, then cover it over with a piece of well-buttered white foolscap or kitchen paper that is cut to fit the stewpan; let the rice cook on the side of the stove for about three quarters of an hour, when all the grains should be quite separate and tender; great care should be taken not to mix it at all with a spoon; the pan itself should be shaken when the grains require mixing. When the rice is cooked turn it out in a pile on the dish and place the poularde on it. Have two or three truffles, six or eight button mushrooms, and about a quarter of a pound of lean ham, tongue, or spiced lean beef cut in shreds like julienne; sprinkle these all over the top of the fowl and here and there on the rice, and serve.

TURBAN OF CHICKEN FILLETS

Take ten or twelve fillets of chicken, pare, beat them slightly, and lard them with bacon on one side.

With the meat from the legs, prepare a quenelle of forcemeat, a little firm; when passed through a sieve, mix in a third of its volume with as much purée of mushrooms. With the two thirds fill a buttered cylindrical dome-shaped mould; poach the *pain* in the bain-marie and turn it out on a cooked flat of paste, cut to the size of an entrée dish.

The *pain* of forcemeat being cooled, mask it with a layer of raw forcemeat, and apply against it the fillets on their unlarded side; wrap up the parts not larded, with thin layers of bacon, push the turban into a moderate oven, and let it be for twelve or fifteen minutes. When taken out of the oven, moisten slightly the larded parts of the fillets, and salamander them; now immediately remove the layers of bacon, carefully wipe the fat off the cylinder, and slip the turban on to a round dish; which warm underneath, then adorn it with a border of English-paste or 'nouille'-paste; and keep it in the warm-closet for a few minutes. Fill the cylinder of the turban with a garnish composed of cocks' combs and truffles; which mask with a little brown sauce, reduced with Madeira, and send up separately the remainder of the sauce. This entrée is dished up, to go on the table.

HAUNCH OF VENISON

Venison should hang in a dry airy place for from ten days to two weeks, according to the weather, and be rubbed dry with a clean coarse cloth, night and morning. When about to dress it, saw off the shank and the chine bones, strip off the skin, and trim off all rough pieces. Make a paste as follows: rub three pounds of sweet dripping into four pounds of flour and a quart of bran; mix it into a stiff paste with hot water; let it stand one hour to get firm; roll it out half an inch thick, and entirely cover the venison with it; make it adhere of an equal thickness all over. Hang the venison before a large solid fire for three-quarters of an hour, near; then withdraw it, and let it roast gradually till done, basting it frequently with dissolved dripping. Allow thirteen minutes to the pound, weighed with the paste on. Half an hour before serving, split the paste with a knife, take it off; dredge the haunch slightly with baked flour, and baste with dissolved butter till done. Place the venison on a very hot dish, the fat uppermost; pour a little of the gravy, made as follows, into the dish, and send to the table immediately. Serve the rest of the gravy and the sweet sauce in tureens. (French beans, plain boiled, should also be served with venison.) To make the gravy, have three pounds of scrag of mutton, half a pound of liver, one kidney, and the venison trimmings, well washed. Put them into a stewpan, with a chopped shallot, half a carrot, sliced, a teaspoonful of salt, one clove, a bayleaf, six peppercorns, two ounces of butter, a dessertspoonful of baked flour, and fry till brown. Add two tablespoonfuls of rum or brandy, a black onion, and a quart of water. Simmer for four hours, skimming frequently. Strain; add a wineglassful of port wine, and serve at once. Dissolve in an enamelled saucepan one pound, or more, of red currant, or ashberry, jelly, and serve in a tureen.

TURKEY HASHED

Cold roast turkey; pepper; salt; half a pint of gravy; a piece of butter the size of a walnut; a little flour; a spoonful of ketchup; peel of half a lemon.

Cut the breast of a cold turkey, or any of the white meat, into thin slices. Cut off the legs, score them, dredge them with pepper and salt, and broil them over a clear fire a nice brown. Put half a pint of gravy into a stewpan with a little piece of butter rolled in flour, a spoonful of ketchup, some pepper and salt, and the peel of half a lemon shred very fine. Put in the turkey, and shake it over a clear fire till it is very hot, place it in a dish with the broiled legs on the top, and sippets of fried bread round it.

POULARDES ENGLISH FASHION

Truss two pullets, as for entrée, with the feet turned under the skin; cover the breast with bacon, place them in a stewpan, strew with trimmings of bacon and vegetables; moisten to height with white broth; cover with buttered paper, and cook them in a moderate oven.

Meanwhile, boil in water two small ox-tongues, to be done at the same time with the pullets; when ready to serve, drain them and remove the skin. Drain also the poulardes, to remove the strings and bacon.

Fix on the centre of an oblong dish a square support of fried bread, but longer than wide; mask each end of the dish next the support with a layer of raw forcemeat, poach it at the mouth of the oven, then dish the poulardes, turning their breasts towards the forcemeat, and resting their backs against the support of bread. Dish the tongues upright on the sides, garnish the intervals, on the right with French beans in lozenges, boiled in water; on the left with small glazed carrots. Garnish each end with a bouquet of cauliflowers in flowrets, boiled in salted water; and insert on the top of the support a hâtelet skewer, simply garnished with large button mushrooms.

Glaze the tongues with a paste-brush, mask slightly the breasts of the poulardes with a little white sauce, prepared with their stock, pouring the remainder into a sauceboat. This dish is arranged to figure on the table; the poulardes should be carved on the sideboard.

MINION-FILLETS OF POULARDE, PARIS-FASHION

This entrée is easy, and less expensive, if, when one of fillets of pullet or chickens has been served the day before, the minion-fillets have been kept for use.

Pick out the inner sinew of the minion-fillets, and remove the superficial epidermis; beat them slightly with the handle of a knife dipped in water; make in them small transversal incisions, into which insert some crescent-shaped truffles, sliced slantwise. The fillets being thus decorated, arrange them in a circle, in a buttered sauté pan; salt slightly, moisten with a paste-brush dipped in melted butter, and put them by.

Prepare a little quenelle forcemeat, with poultry meat and the trimmings of the fillets. Butter the interior of a pyramid-mould, mask the bottom and sides with a layer of previously-prepared forcemeat, about a third of an inch thick; fill the hollow of the mould with a ragout of poultry-livers, mixed with a few sliced truffles, and thickened with a few spoonfuls of brown sauce, reduced with Madeira; the ragout should be cold; cover it with a layer of forcemeat, and poach the *pain* in the bain-marie for three quarters of an hour.

When ready to serve, fry the minion-fillets on a brisk fire, only for a few seconds, thus setting them; drain immediately dry, and dish them up in a circular order, round the poached *pain* of forcemeat, meanwhile turned out on the centre of a dish; which mask slightly, as well as the bottom of it, with a little good white sauce; and insert on the top a hâtelet-skewer, garnished with a nice cock's comb and a truffle.

This dish is placed on a hot-water dish.

PHEASANT A LA BELLE ALLIANCE

[A Sportsman's Dish; very expensive, except for Country Gentlemen.]

One pheasant; two woodcocks; four snipes; half a bottle of truffles; one bouquet of mixed herbs; pepper and salt, of each one teaspoonful; a good pinch of cayenne; half a bottle of sherry.

Select a fine cock pheasant, bone it, have ready the flesh of two woodcocks and four snipes pounded well in a mortar; add to this, panada, half a bottle of truffles, the bouquet of herbs chopped very fine, and a high seasoning. Stuff the pheasant with the forcemeat thus made, lay it on the spit, and baste it with sherry. Serve it up on toast with the trails of the woodcocks and snipes, with chopped truffles spread on it.

MAYONNAISE OF CHICKEN IN SHELLS

Have china or plated scallop shells for these; place about one teaspoonful of thick mayonnaise sauce in the centre of each shell;

take the remains of cold chicken and cut it in little neat pieces about the size of a halfpenny piece, also little crisp pieces of lettuce and slices of hardboiled egg, fillets of boned anchovies, and stoned olives. Arrange these alternately on the sauce, forming a nice pile, then cover all up with mayonnaise sauce, and smooth the top with a knife. Cook some chicken livers in a little butter for about ten minutes in the oven, with a paper over, and season with a little pepper and salt; rub the livers, when cool, through a wire sieve, and then sprinkle it lightly over the mayonnaise: have the hard-boiled yolk of egg likewise passed through the sieve and lightly sprinkled on the liver, and also a little chopped tarragon and chervil or parsley. Place four little bunches of French capers on the edge of the mayonnaise, and on the top of each coquille put two neat fillets of boned anchovies, with a little strip of French gherkin or beetroot between the fillets. Serve one to each person; dish on a napkin or paper.

CRÊPINETTES A LA DESBOROUGH

Take the remains of some cold game or poultry, free it from skin and bone, and cut it into neat little slices with some cooked button mushrooms and truffle. Prepare a farce as below, put it into a forcing bag with a plain pipe, and force out about a teaspoonful of it on to a stamped-out round of cooked ox-tongue or lean ham; make little wells in the centre of the farce, and arrange some of the pieces of game, etc., in the spaces, pressing them carefully in; put on the top of this about a saltspoonful of the sauce, prepared as below, then brush over with a little raw white of egg, and wrap each in a small piece of cleansed and dried pork caul; brush this over with the raw white of egg, then put the crêpinettes in a well-buttered sauté pan with a buttered paper over, place the pan in a tin containing boiling water, put this in a moderate oven, and cook the contents for about fifteen minutes; then take up, brush over the crêpinettes with a little warm thin glaze, arrange them on a border of purée of potato that has been forced on to a dish by means of a forcing bag and a large rose pipe, and serve with Desborough sauce (as below) round the dish. Use whilst quite hot for an entrée.

FARCE FOR CRÊPINETTES

Pound till smooth a quarter of a pound of raw game or poultry with two ounces of fat and lean fresh pork or bacon and two ounces of cooked ox-tongue, then add to it a wineglassful of sherry, a saltspoonful of extract of meat, two raw eggs, and a little salt and pepper; rub all through a fine wire sieve and mix in it in a pan or basin a finely chopped shallot and a little finely chopped parsley, and use.

SAUCE FOR CENTRE OF CRÊPINETTES

Put into a stewpan one finely chopped shallot, one ounce of glaze, the pulp of one large ripe tomato, a saltspoonful of chopped chutney, as much curry powder as will cover a sixpenny piece, one tablespoonful of good brown sauce, two tablespoonfuls of oyster liquor, and a few drops of strained lemon juice; boil till reduced to a thick creamy consistency, then add to it three raw sauce oysters that have been bearded and cut up into tiny dice shapes; set the mixture aside until cold, then use.

DESBOROUGH SAUCE

Take a quarter of a pint of white wine, a quarter of a pint of tomato purée, one ounce of glaze, two finely chopped shallots, half a pint of good game or poultry gravy, a quarter of a pint of oyster liquor, two bayleaves, a sprig of thyme, one fresh mushroom, a dust of coralline pepper, and a few drops of carmine; boil for about fifteen minutes, then stir on to one ounce of arrowroot that has been mixed with a wineglass of mushroom liquor or sherry, add a pinch of salt and a few drops of lemon juice, then use.

CUTLETS OF PIGEON A LA ROSALIND

Bone some pigeons, but leave the feet and leg bones attached; cut them into halves, season with salt, pepper, finely chopped mushroom, lean cooked ham or tongue, raw parsley, and shallot;

place them in a buttered sauté pan and fry over a quick fire for four or five minutes, then take up and put them between two plates and set them aside until cold. Mask each with the farce prepared as below, using a bag and pipe for the purpose, smooth over the farce with a hot wet knife, arrange shreds of French gherkin and little diamond shapes of truffle on the farce, brush over with raw white of egg, and wrap up the pigeons in pork caul; brush them over again with white of egg, place them in a well-buttered sauté pan with a buttered paper over, and cook in a moderate oven for about fifteen minutes; when cooked take up and arrange the birds on a border of potato, in the centre of which has been placed a croûton of fried bread; garnish between each bird with a purée of flageolets or peas, pour the sauce prepared as below round the base, fix two hâtelet skewers in the top and serve for a hot entrée.

SAUCE FOR CUTLETS OF PIGEONS

Put into a stewpan the bones and any trimmings from the birds, two finely chopped shallots, one ounce of butter, and a little strip of lean raw bacon; fry these together for fifteen minutes, add two wineglassfuls of white wine, one and a half pints of light chicken or veal gravy, a teaspoonful of extract of meat, half a pint of mushroom liquor, and a few fresh mushroom stalks; let the mixture simmer for forty minutes, strain it, and add one pint of the liquor to two ounces of butter and the same quantity of fine flour that have been fried together without browning; also add a quarter of a pint of cream, the juice of a lemon, a few drops of carmine, and one ounce of grated Parmesan cheese; bring to the boil, then tammy, re-warm in a bain-marie, and use.

FARCE FOR CUTLETS OF PIGEONS

Pound together two ounces of raw veal, rabbit or chicken, and three ounces of lean cooked ham, mix with this two ounces of pounded panard, two raw yolks and one white of egg, and two tablespoonfuls of purée prepared as below; rub the whole through a wire sieve and use.

PURÉE FOR CUTLETS OF PIGEONS

Put into a stewpan two raw ripe tomatoes, one chopped shallot, two bayleaves, a sprig of thyme, one split capsicum, a dust of coralline pepper, a pinch of salt, a teaspoonful of extract of meat, and half a wineglassful of sherry; colour with carmine to the desired shade, boil to quite a thick pulp, then mix with the farce.

CUTLETS OF PHEASANT A L'INDIENNE

Prepare a farce as below, and with it fill some little buttered cutlet moulds that have been ornamented with a little chopped truffle; when filled knock the moulds on the table so that the farce sinks well into the shapes, make a little well in the centre of each with the finger, which should be occasionally dipped in hot water, and in the spaces thus formed place about a saltspoonful of the sauce prepared as below, cover over with a little more of the farce, and then place the moulds in a sauté pan on a piece of paper; cover them with good-flavoured light stock, watch them come to the boil, then draw the pan to the side of the stove, cover it up, and let the contents poach for fifteen minutes; then take up, turn out the cutlets, and drain them. Dish them on a border of potato, and garnish the centre with peas or other nice green vegetables; pour the sauce round the base, and serve hot for an entrée.

FARCE FOR CUTLETS

Take twelve ounces of pheasant and pound it till smooth, then pound eight ounces of panard with one ounce of butter, and a pinch of salt and coralline pepper; mix together with three whole raw eggs and rub through a fine wire sieve; then add two table-spoonfuls of thick cream, and use.

SAUCE FOR INSIDE CUTLETS

Put into a stewpan a teaspoonful of extract of meat, one table-spoonful of good brown sauce, a dust of coralline pepper, a teaspoonful of chopped chutney, a saltspoonful of French mustard, the same of English mustard, six or eight drops of lemon juice, and a quarter of an ounce of powder; boil these ingredients together, add the purée of one large boiled onion that has been rubbed through a sieve, mix well together, set it aside on ice until firm, then use.

SAUCE FOR SERVING ROUND CUTLETS

Fry four peeled and finely sliced onions in one and a half ounces of good butter till a nice golden colour with the bones from the pheasant and a bunch of herbs, then mix with two ounces of butter and the same quantity of flour that have been fried together without discolouring; add one pint of good-flavoured light stock, and stir together till the mixture boils, then add the juice of a lemon, a teaspoonful of curry powder, a pinch of salt, and half a gill of thick cream; let it simmer for twenty minutes, remove the bones, tammy, and use.

LITTLE BOMBES OF GAME A LA MARSEILLE

Take half a pound of cooked bird freed from bone and skin and pound it until smooth, then mix with it a quarter pound of pounded panard, two tablespoonfuls of reduced espagnol sauce, three raw yolks and one white of egg, a few drops of carmine, and a little salt and coralline pepper; rub it through a fine wire sieve and put the mixture into a forcing bag with a plain pipe and force it out into little buttered bombe moulds that have been garnished in any pretty design with stamped-out pieces of hard-boiled white of egg sprinkled with chopped parsley and little shreds of cooked cucumber; make a little well in the centre of each with the finger, which should occasionally be dipped into hot water; then fill up the spaces thus formed with the purée as below, poach the bombes for twenty minutes, then turn them out of the moulds, mask them with the sauce prepared as below, and arrange them on a purée of potato that has been forced on to the dish through a forcing pipe with a large rose pipe. Serve for an entrée for a dinner party.

PURÉE FOR BOMBES

Take four or five large fresh mushrooms, wash, and press them dry, and chop them finely, put them into a stewpan with one ounce of butter, a little salt and white pepper, and one chopped shallot; draw them down on the stove until into a pulp, then mix with two tablespoonfuls of finely chopped cooked game, one ounce of finely chopped lean ham, a teaspoonful of extract of meat, and a pinch of chopped parsley; stir till boiling, then set it aside until somewhat cool, then mix with one whole beaten-up egg, and use.

SAUCE FOR BOMBES

Put into a stewpan one pint of good light stock, any bones from the bird, two chopped shallots, three raw ripe tomatoes, a bunch of herbs (thyme, parsley, and bayleaf), a pinch of mignonette pepper, a few drops of carmine, a teaspoonful of extract of meat, boil for fifteen minutes, then stir into it half an ounce of cornflour, stir till re-boiling, remove any bones, then rub the sauce through a tammy, re-warm, and use.

EGG GARNISH

Take two raw whites of eggs, a teaspoonful of cream, a little salt; mix together with a fork until smooth, poach it in moulds till firm, stamp out in the desired shapes, and use.

CUCUMBER SHREDS

Cut some raw cucumbers into fine shreds, the length of the moulds, put them into cold water, bring to the boil, simmer them until tender, strain them, and use when cold.

CROUSTADES OF LARKS A LA ROTHSCHILD

Cut either round or square croustades from a stale household loaf, making each large enough to hold a lark when scooped out. Make an inner ring or square on the top of each, cutting it about a quarter of an inch deep; fry the croustades in clean boiling fat until of a golden colour, then remove the inner rings or squares from the tops without breaking them, and scoop out the soft insides and put a lark prepared as below in each, fill up the croustades with Rothschild sauce, replace the tops, and garnish with little rings of fried bread arranged round the top of the croustades. To prepare the larks, cleanse, singe and bone them, filling them with pâté de foie gras. Place a band of buttered paper round each bird, put them in a lightly buttered sauté pan, with a thin slice of fat bacon on the breast of each, and moisten with a wineglass of sherry. Cook for about twelve minutes in a moderate oven with a buttered paper over, basting the birds occasionally, then remove the papers, put the birds into the croustades, and cover with the sauce.

ROTHSCHILD SAUCE

Chop the bones of the larks and put them in a buttered stewpan with one large fresh mushroom, half an onion sliced, a bunch of herbs, and a pinch of mignonette pepper; fry for a quarter of an hour, then add a wineglass of sherry, the liquor from the larks, three quarters of a pint of thick brown sauce, one ounce of good glaze, and a pinch of castor sugar. Boil together for about a quarter of an hour, keeping it skimmed while the sauce is boiling, then strain and tammy, and add the essence from a bottle of truffles and two or three truffles finely shredded, and use.

GALANTINE OF CHICKEN

Bone the bird and season it inside with coralline pepper and salt. Prepare as below a forcemeat of veal or fresh pork chopped very fine and passed through a mincing machine, and season this well; place it out about one inch thick on a slab, arrange on this strips of cooked bacon or ham and tongue, blanched pistachio nuts, almonds, and truffles. Roll up the forcemeat and carefully push it into the boned bird at the neck end, using a little cold water while doing so to bind the meat. Butter a cloth and tie the galantine up in it, and cook it in stock with herbs and vegetables such as thyme, parsley, bayleaf, basil, and marjoram, a few peppercorns, carrots, turnips, leeks, celery, etc., for about one and a half to two hours according to size, then remove from the cloth and tie it up again to tighten it, and put it to press until quite cold and firm. Dish up and garnish with truffle and aspic to taste. If wished to look well, arrange it on a croûton or a block of rice. Galantines of any game or poultry are made in a similar manner.

FORCEMEAT FOR GALANTINE

For a moderate-sized fowl take ten ounces of lean veal, twelve ounces of fresh pork, a quarter of a pound of ham, a quarter of a pound of tongue, twenty-four pistachio nuts, twelve almonds, three or four truffles, about six or eight turned olives, and five or six boned anchovies if liked.

CAKES & BREAD

FRENCH BREAD

Put one pound of fine flour in a basin, and in another vessel put three tablespoonfuls of milk and the same of water; make this just tepid and then mix with it one ounce of German yeast, one ounce of butter, and a saltspoonful of salt; make a well in the centre of the flour and pour the yeast mixture into it, sprinkle over with a little of the flour, cover the basin over with a cloth, and leave it in a warm place for three hours; then knead it up into a light dough with one and a half gills of tepid milk and water; cover the dough again and leave it in a warm place for another half hour, then turn the dough out on to a slab or table and make into any fancy shapes; put these on a lightly floured tin and put aside on the screen to rise for about ten minutes, then bake in a moderate oven for fifteen to twenty minutes. As this bread requires a considerable time to make, it can (if required to be served hot for breakfast) be baked the previous day and heated the next morning; to make it hot brush over the top lightly with warm milk, place it on a hot baking tin and cover it over with a damp sheet of kitchen paper; stand it in a moderate oven for about ten minutes, then take up and dish in a pile.

JUBILEE TEA CAKES

Put half a gill of cream and half a gill of water into a stewpan with two ounces of fresh butter and one ounce of castor sugar, and let it come to the boil; then mix into it three ounces of very finely chopped almonds; work these well together and let it cook on the side of the stove for about five minutes; put four raw yolks of eggs and a few drops of essence of vanilla into a basin and work it well for about ten minutes, then stir the almond mixture gradually into the yolks, mix well for five minutes, then whip the whites of two raw eggs quite stiff with a pinch of salt, and mix them into the prepared mixture. Lightly butter and paper a round fleur ring and dust it with castor sugar and fine flour mixed in equal quantities; put a sheet of buttered paper on a baking tin, pour the mixture into the ring, and bake for about twenty-five minutes. The cakes should be a pale brown colour when baked; take them from the oven, remove the paper, place them on a pastry rack, and when cold glaze them with tea glacé, and before the glacé is set sprinkle the top with blanched and shredded pistachios, and garnish round the edge with desiccated coconut. Serve on a dish-paper or napkin for tea or dessert, or for a sweet for luncheon or with a compote of fruit or ice. The chopped almonds are better if passed through a sieve.

COFFEE CAKES

Put into a stewpan four whole raw eggs, half a tablespoonful of strong coffee or coffee essence, and six ounces of castor sugar, and whip all together over boiling water till just warm; take off and continue the whipping till the mixture is cold and stiff, then add by degrees four ounces of fine flour, which have been passed through a sieve and made warm, one ounce of crême de riz, and one eighth of an ounce of baking powder; take any little fancy tins, such as are used for sponge cakes, finger biscuits, etc., and first brush over the insides with warm butter, and then dust them over with a little castor sugar and fine flour mixed in equal quantities; after the tins have been thus dusted, knock them on the table to remove any superfluous flour and sugar, fill them with cake mixture and bake for about fifteen minutes and then turn them out. These can be served plain with a little castor sugar dusted over them, or may be glazed with coffee glacé.

GÂTEAU A LA TROUVILLE

Prepare a sponge mixture, as follows: To four ounces of castor sugar add four eggs; heat over boiling water until luke-warm, then remove and whip till cold and stiff, and add, by degrees, three ounces of fine flour that has been passed through the sieve, and one-eighth of an ounce of baking powder; have the half of a melon mould rubbed over well with cold butter and dusted over with sifted flour. Fill it with the mixture, put a band of buttered paper round and place it in a moderate oven for about thirty-five to forty minutes; when the cake looks a pretty golden colour, put a piece of paper over the top, and care must be taken to prevent the bottom of the cake getting discoloured, say by placing an extra baking tin under it. When the cake is cooked turn it out, and when cool scoop out the inside of the cake and rest it in a basin or mould, nearly fill up the hollow with apricot or any other fruit purée, cut the bottom slice off the piece scooped out of the cake and fix this over the purée to keep it in when the cake is turned over; glaze all over with coffee glacé, and when cold dish on a border of vanilla ice cream (prepared as below); when the glacé is set, make incisions all over, and put in them shredded pistachio, dried cherries, and almonds.

VANILLA CREAM ICED FOR BORDER

Freeze one and a half pints of single cream, flavoured with vanilla and half a wineglass of white rum, and sweetened with four ounces of castor sugar, then put it in a border mould large enough to rest the cake on, and stand it in the ice cave for about one and a half hours; when sufficiently set turn out on a dish-paper on the dish it is to be served on, and on this place the cake, and serve.

MELON A L'IMPÉRATRICE

Take half a pound of butter, half a pound of baked almonds chopped fine, six ounces of crême de riz, two saltspoonfuls of apple green, six whole raw eggs, four ounces of castor sugar, a wineglass of white rum, two saltspoonfuls of essence of vanilla; work the butter till like a cream, then add the crême de riz, sugar, colouring, and the eggs by degrees, and finally the almonds and one-eighth of an ounce of baking powder, and work all together for about fifteen minutes. Butter and flour the two halves of the melon mould, and half fill them with the above paste, bake for about half to three quarters of an hour in a moderate oven; turn the cakes out of the mould; when they are cool trim them off evenly, so that when put together they will form a ball; scoop out the centres and fill the spaces with apricot or strawberry jam and whipped cream, sweetened and flavoured with vanilla; place the two parts together, glaze the cake with noyau or maraschino glacé coloured with a little apple green, dish on a border of nougat on a paper, garnish with leaves, and serve.

METTERNICH CAKE

Take four whole raw eggs, six ounces of castor sugar, a pinch of cinnamon, and the very finely chopped peel of a lemon; whip these all together in a stewpan over boiling water till the mixture is just warm; then remove and whip till cold and thick, and mix into it four ounces of warm fine flour that has been passed through a sieve, and one eighth of an ounce of baking powder. Butter a square fleur mould, place it on a baking tin, and put a double layer of buttered paper on the bottom inside the mould; then pour

4—TVCB * *

in the mixture, and bake in a moderate oven for one hour. The cake should be a very pale fawn colour when cooked.

Prepare a similar quantity of the above mixture, but in addition add about a saltspoonful of cherry red or carmine and a few drops of essence of vanilla, and finish as for the first mixture.

When both mixtures are cold cut them in slices and arrange them together in alternate layers, placing between each slice a layer of Vienna chocolate icing that is mixed with a wineglass of white rum; when they have reached the required height mask over with maraschino glacé and then dish on a cake bottom. Garnish the cake as in the engraving with Vienna chocolate icing and rose Vienna icing, and serve. This would be nice to serve for a dinner sweet when ice cream or fruits may be served with it.

FORTRESS OF BISCUITS

Work well in a kitchen-basin a pound of powder-sugar, flavoured with orange, with four whole eggs, and twelve yolks of eggs; the preparation being frothy, gradually introduce into it a little more than three quarters of a pound of melted butter, clarified; continue working. A few minutes after, introduce into it four tablespoonfuls of rum, a little salt, then five or six whipped whites of eggs, as well as half a pound of flour, or potato-flour, passed through a sieve.

Take a tin-case, the height and width intended for the fortress; butter its inside with clarified butter, and glaze it with fine sugar; set it on a round thick baking-sheet covered with buttered paper; fill it, nearly to its height, with the previously prepared biscuit-paste; which now bake, in a moderate oven, for one hour and a quarter. Bake the remainder of the paste in a flat stewpan, being an inch and a quarter larger than the tin-case.

The biscuit of the tin-case being turned out, and cooled, cut it straight, then diminish its thickness, from the bottom up to about three quarters of its height, so as to leave on the top a border in relief; now slightly empty out the top, so as to give the upper circle of the top a thickness of but one-third of an inch; by aid of a little knife cut the upper border into battlements; the biscuit may be cut very neatly. Now pierce the sides of the paste in imitation of loop-holes, two of which are furnished with guns imitated in biscuit. Of these guns nothing is to be seen but the muzzles, they are fixed on their place at the last moment.

With a clear icing-sugar perfumed with orange-zest, and slightly coloured, mask all the surface of the biscuit, set it on a pastry-grille; adorn the sides of the biscuit with white icing-sugar, squeezed through a cornet, so as to imitate the hewn stones of a fortress.

Hollow the dish-biscuit, leaving the sides more than half an inch thick; cut these sides into battlements, in the same manner as the upper border, and likewise mask them with icing sugar. The icing sugar being dry, slip the bottom on a dish, place the large biscuit in the centre, garnish its inside with a *plombière* cream, that is, with ice-vanilla, mixed up with whipped cream.

POTATO MUFFINS

Three large mealy potatoes; a little salt; two ounces of butter; two eggs; a small teaspoonful of soda; a teacupful of yeast; three pints of flour; one pint of warm water.

Boil and mash three large mealy potatoes, and beat them smooth with about two ounces of butter and a little salt, adding sufficient warm water to make it the consistency of very thick cream. Well beat two eggs, mix them in, and then stir to the whole three pints of fine dried and sifted flour; mix these well together and add a pint of lukewarm water, then stir in the soda and yeast, and set it to rise all night. The next morning bake the muffins in rings on a griddle.

JUMBLES

A pound and a half of flour; three-quarters of a pound of butter; half a pound of sugar; three eggs; a quarter of a grated nutmeg; half a teaspoonful of lemon extract, or of ground cinnamon.

Work three-quarters of a pound of butter into a pound and a half of flour, half a pound of sugar, and three well-beaten eggs; add a quarter of a nutmeg grated, a little lemon extract, or ground cinnamon. Mix it all well together, and then roll it out to an eighth of an inch in thickness, grate loaf sugar over it, cut it into round cakes, make an aperture in the centre of each, lay them on tin plates, and bake them ten minutes in a quick oven.

WINE CAKES

Eight ounces of flour; half a pound of sugar; a quarter of a pound of butter; one wineglassful of wine; four eggs; a few caraway seeds.

Mix eight ounces of flour with half a pound of finely powdered sugar; beat four ounces of fresh butter with a glass of wine, then make the flour and sugar into a paste with it, and four eggs beaten light, add a few caraway seeds, and roll the paste as thin as paper. Cut the cakes with the top of a tumbler, brush the tops over with the beaten white of an egg, grate sugar over, and bake them ten or twelve minutes in a quick oven. Take them from the tins when cold.

SAVOURY PIES
&
PUDDINGS

FRENCH RAISED GAME PIE

Prepare a raised pie paste, and with it line a French raised pie
mould to scarcely a quarter of an inch thick; then prepare a farce
or mince as follows: Take ten ounces of veal, twelve ounces of
fresh pork, and chop very fine, or pass twice through a mincing
machine; season with coralline pepper, salt, and arrange this on
the paste in the mould. Fill in with fillets of pigeon, chicken, or
any game you may have, strips of tongue, ham, or bacon, hard-
boiled yolks of eggs that are masked with chopped parsley and
seasoned with pepper and salt, button mushrooms, pistachios,
truffles, pâté de foie gras, cocks' combs, and any farced birds, such
as larks, quails, or ortolans, so as to stand higher than the mould;
cover in with more of the farce or mince, and then put a somewhat
thinner layer of paste over the top, first wetting the edges of the
paste round the mould, press the edges together, and trim off the
paste; brush the top lightly with cold water, stamp out some
rounds of the paste and work them into leaves or other pretty
designs, and ornament the top of the pie with them; fix a buttered
paper round the mould standing some six inches higher than the
top of the pie. Bake gently for about two and a half to three hours,
taking care that the paste is not browned, as it should be a rich

fawn colour when done; when cooked put the pie aside in the mould till it is cold, then remove the top by cutting the paste through round the edge of the mould, and fill up the pie with any nice meat jelly that is not quite set, and put aside again until the jelly is quite set; then cover the top with some chopped aspic and replace the paste cover. Remove the mould, dish on a paper, and it may be garnished round with aspic jelly. Care must be taken when filling up the mould that the jelly is not too liquid or it will go through the paste. This is excellent as a side dish, or for wedding breakfasts, ball suppers, and, in fact, for use generally.

BEEF AND LARK PUDDING

Have eighteen or twenty larks picked and boned; season them with a little coralline pepper, a little salt, finely chopped herbs (parsley, thyme and bayleaf), and two or three washed fresh mushrooms chopped (the tinned mushrooms can be used if the fresh are not to be procured). Cut up one pound and a half of fillet or rump steak in little square pieces about half the size of the boned larks; rub six boned and filleted anchovies through a sieve, and mix this and the larks and the meat together, and sprinkle a tablespoonful of fine flour over all. Prepare a suet crust and with it line a buttered basin or plain mould to about one third of an inch thick, pressing the paste well to the basin or mould; fill it in with the larks and beef, leaving enough room to put in a pint of cold water or ordinary stock free from fat; wet round the edge of the paste with a little cold water, cover over with paste, press the edges together, trim off any superfluous paste, tie a cloth over the top, and put the basin or mould in a pot containing boiling water sufficient to cover it, and let it boil on steadily for five to six hours; take it up, remove the cloth, run a knife round between the paste and the edge of the basin, and turn the pudding out on to a very hot dish, and sprinkle the top with a little finely chopped parsley, truffle, or coralline pepper.

ASPARAGUS PUDDING

Two dessertspoonfuls of minced ham; a little milk; half a pint of asparagus; three dessertspoonfuls of flour; four eggs.

Mince a little lean ham very fine, and mix it with four well-beaten eggs, a seasoning of pepper and salt, a little flour, and a piece of butter the size of a walnut. Cut the green parts of the asparagus into very small pieces, not larger than a pea, and mix all together. Then add a sufficient quantity of fresh milk to make the mixture the consistency of fresh butter, and put it into a well-buttered mould that will just hold it; dredge a cloth with flour, tie it over the pudding, and put it into a saucepan of boiling water. When done, turn it out carefully on to a dish, and pour some good melted butter round it.

VEAL PUDDING

One pound and a half of veal; three slices of bacon; a piece of butter the size of an egg; pepper and salt; a small bunch of thyme; two or three spoonfuls of water; suet paste.

Cut about two pounds of lean veal into small collops a quarter of an inch in thickness, put a piece of butter the size of an egg into a very clean frying pan to melt, then lay in the veal and a few slices of bacon, a small sprig of thyme, and a seasoning of pepper and salt, place the pan over a slow fire for about ten minutes then add two or three spoonfuls of warm water. Just boil it up, and then let it stand to cool. Line a pudding-basin with a good suet crust, lay in the veal and bacon, pour the gravy over it, roll out a piece of paste to form a lid, place it over, press it close with the thumb, tie the basin in a pudding-cloth, and put it into a saucepan of boiling water, keeping it continually boiling until done.

YORKSHIRE CHRISTMAS PIE

One turkey; one goose; one fowl; one pigeon; a little sausage meat; some forcemeat; six or eight hardboiled eggs; half an ounce of pepper; half an ounce of salt; and some savoury jelly or gravy; enough raised pie-crust.

Bone a turkey, a goose, a fowl, and a pigeon, and season the insides of each with pepper and salt mixed together. Put the goose inside the turkey, the fowl inside the goose, and the pigeon inside that, filling the interstices with a little forcemeat, sausage meat, and six or eight hard-boiled eggs cut into three. Sew up the turkey to give the appearance of a whole bird, and lay it in a thick raised crust. Cut or mark out a lid at the top, brush it over with the beaten yolk of eggs, and ornament the top and sides. Bake it in a slow oven, and then carefully raise the lid and pour in some savoury gravy or jelly, and let it stand to cool.

It will keep a long time, as the crust is not to be eaten, but merely forms a case for the poultry.

SMALL RAISED YORKSHIRE PORK PIES

Two pounds of neck of pork; a quarter of a pound of butter; a quarter of a pound of suet; one pound of flour; a teaspoonful of sage; pepper and salt.

Chop a quarter of a pound of suet very fine, mix it with a quarter of a pound of butter, and a pound of fine dry flour, and put it in a stewpan over a slow fire to become hot, and the suet and butter melted. Then knead it into a very stiff paste, and set it before the fire covered over with a cloth until required. Cut the pork into the smallest pieces and season them highly with pepper, salt, and a teaspoonful of powdered sage. Divide the paste into as many pieces as you think fit, reserving some for the tops; raise them into round forms, fill them with the small pieces of seasoned pork, cover the tops over, pinch them round with your thumb and finger, and bake them in a very hot brick oven.

RICH RABBIT PIE

One rabbit; a quarter of a pound of ham, or bacon; pepper, salt and a little pounded mace; four hardboiled eggs; some forcemeat balls; a large cupful of good stock or gravy; puff paste.

Cut up and bone a young rabbit; put the bones into a stewpan with a few herbs, pepper, salt, and any trimmings you may have. Just cover it with water, and let it simmer to about half a pint. Put a puff paste round the edge of a pie-dish, put the slices of rabbit in, then the bacon or ham, hardboiled eggs cut into pieces and some forcemeat balls. Season the whole with pepper, salt and pounded mace, pour in a cupful of stock or water, cover the top with a good puff paste, make a hole with the knife in the top, and bake it in a rather hot oven, taking care it does not gain too much colour. When done, pour through the hole at the top the gravy made from the bones, and serve.

COLD SNIPE PIE

Choose a channelled pie-mould of low shape; butter its interior, set it on a round baking-sheet, covered with buttered paper. Prepare two pounds of common short-paste; let it rest for two hours.

Bone seven or eight wood-snipes, or three woodcocks, remove the skin from the meat, put them into a kitchen-basin, add to them a pound of raw truffles, cut in dice, moisten with four tablespoonfuls of Madeira. Take the snipes' livers and trails, add to them a few raw poultry-livers; fry them together, with melted bacon, on a brisk fire; season highly, let them cool, pound, and pass them through a sieve.

Take the meat of four hares' legs, remove the tough parts, cut the meat in pieces, which immediately fry with bacon; season them, pound, and pass them through a sieve; which then mix into the previously strained purée. On the other hand, prepare some raw mince, with lean veal or fresh pork (taking about two pounds) half and half, mixed with the same of fresh bacon. Season the mince, pound, pass it through a sieve; put it into a basin, then add to it the purée of cooked meat.

Line the mould with paste, then mask this paste with a thick layer of the prepared forcemeat. Place in the centre the pieces of snipe and truffle, with alternate layers of the same forcemeat. Raise the preparation in a dome. Cover the pie with paste, adorn it tastefully; egg it on the top, bake it in a moderate oven for two hours, carefully covering it with paper. Half an hour after taking it out of the oven, infilter into it, through the top, a few table-spoonfuls of aspic-jelly, mixed with a little Madeira.

The pie represented by the drawing is dished on a napkin. The top is not open, as on the centre of the dome, on the summit of which is left during cooking time an aperture for the evaporation of steam, is placed the head of a snipe with the plumage on. For the sake of solidity the neck must be cut off, and the hollow filled with a piece of carrot, traversed by a bit of iron wire.

VEAL AND HAM PIE

Two pounds of veal cutlets; half a pound of ham; one ounce and a half of butter; a sprig of parsley; pepper and salt; a tablespoonful of ketchup; four or five mushrooms; six hardboiled eggs; a large cupful of water or gravy and a little flour; three quarters of a pound of puff paste.

Cut about two pounds of veal and half a pound of ham or bacon into rather small cutlets; fry three or four minced mushrooms and a sprig of parsley in a small piece of butter seasoned with pepper and salt. Then pour in a tablespoonful of ketchup, about half a pint of water (or gravy if you have it), dredge in some flour, and stir it all over the fire till it boils; place the veal and ham alternately in a pie-dish lined with puff paste, make a hole at the top, ornament it with paste in any form you please, and bake it. Pour in a little more gravy, when done, through the hole at the top.

SHRIMP PIE

One quart or more of shrimps; one glass of white wine; two anchovies; half a blade of mace; one clove; two ounces of butter; puff paste.

When the shrimps are picked, season them with half a blade of mace and one clove pounded, mixed with two anchovies chopped very fine. Put a paste round the edge of a pie-dish, and a few pieces of butter at the bottom, then put in the shrimps and more butter, pour in a glass of white wine. Cover it with a puff paste, glaze it, and bake.

SALMON PIE, RAISED

Two pounds of salmon; pepper; salt; mace; and nutmeg; a little melted butter; and one pound and a half of raised pie paste.

Line a well-buttered pie-mould with about a pound of paste, pressing it carefully round the interior; boil two pounds of salmon, and when done, take off the skin and remove the bones; pound it in a mortar seasoned with salt, pepper, nutmeg, and a very little pounded mace. Then place the salmon in the mould, cover it over with paste, cutting out of the top a piece to form a lid, and pressing the paste closely over; cover the lid over it, brush it with the yolk of a beaten egg, and carve it round the edge with any device you like. When done, lift up the lid, and pour in some butter nicely melted. Serve with, and lay a few slices of, lemon over it.

RAISED PIE PASTE

Put two pounds and a half of fine flour on a pasteboard, and put into a stewpan three-quarters of a pint of water with four ounces of

butter and four ounces of lard. When the water boils, make a
hole in the middle of the flour, pour in the water, butter and lard
by degrees, gently mixing the whole with a wooden spoon. When
it is mixed well, knead it with your hands till it becomes stiff,
dredging it with a little flour to prevent it sticking to the board.
When thoroughly kneaded, put it into a pan, cover it over with a
cloth, and set it before the fire for five or six minutes, when it will
be fit for use.

GAME PIE FOR A HUNTING BREAKFAST

One goose; one turkey; one snipe; one grouse; two woodcocks;
one pheasant; two partridges; one and a half bullock's tongues,
and half the meat of one hare; one pint of good gravy; one pound
of grated ham; seven pounds of flour; one and a quarter pounds
of suet; two pounds of butter.

Make an ornamental crust with the flour, suet and butter, in a
fancy shape, with a top to fit, and bake it in a slow oven. Cut all
the game and bullock's tongue into small pieces, and stew them
gently. Put it into the crust, adding the gravy and grated ham
(cooked), and a little seasoning if required. Cover with the paste
top, and warm in a slow oven.

YORKSHIRE PIE

Bone a goose and a large fowl. Fill the latter with a stuffing made
of minced ham or tongue, veal, suet, parsley, pepper, salt and two
eggs; or for a more highly-seasoned stuffing say – minced ham,
veal, suet, onion, sweet-herbs, lemon-peel, mixed spices, cayenne,
salt, worked into a paste with a couple of eggs. Sew up the fowl,
truss it, and stew it for twenty minutes along with the goose in
some good stock, and in a close stewpan. Put the fowl within the
goose, and place the goose in a pie-mould which has been lined
with good hot-water paste. Let the goose repose on a cushion of
stuffing, and in the midst of the liquor in which he has been

stewed. Surround him in the pie with slices of parboiled tongue and pieces of pigeon, partridge or hare. Fill the vacancies with more stuffing; put on a good layer of butter; roof it with paste; bake it for three hours; and consume it either hot or cold. These pies are sometimes made of enormous size, containing every variety of poultry or game, one within another and side by side.

VEAL PIE

Take the back ribs or neck, get rid of all the bone – which should never enter into a pie – and trim the meat into small collops. At the same time cut some streaky bacon into thin slices. Fry the veal and the bacon with a faggot of Duxelles [*Ed:* bouquet garni] in about an ounce of butter. Then lay them in order in a pie-dish intermixed with forcemeat balls and hard-boiled yolks of eggs – it may be also with a scalded sweetbread cut into pieces. Let all be seasoned with pepper and salt, and moistened with half a pint of gravy, to which the juice of half a lemon may be added. Cover it with paste; bake it for an hour or an hour and a quarter; and when the pie is done, lift the top ornament and pour in some good gravy.

SWEETS
&
SWEET PUDDINGS

RICE A LA PARISIENNE

Take a deep plain border mould, line the top with dried cherries
and angelica, cut each cherry in four or six slices, and with the
finger form them into a half-moon shape; stamp out little rounds
of angelica with a small round cutter, or cut it with a knife into
diamond shapes; set the fruit with a little lemon jelly; also line the
mould round the sides with the same jelly. If the mould is to be
enough for eight persons, put three ounces of Carolina rice to
blanch in cold water; when it comes to the boil strain off and
wash it in cold water; put it to cook in a pint of new milk, with
one bayleaf and a piece of cinnamon about one inch in length, and
four ounces of loaf or castor sugar; cook gently on the side of the
stove until the rice has become quite tender and the milk reduced
to about a quarter of a pint, and while the rice is quite hot dissolve
in it rather better than a quarter of an ounce of gelatine; if more
flavour is liked, about six drops of essence of vanilla or a little
vanilla sugar may be used; put it out in a basin, and whilst it is
cooling add half a pint of whipped cream, and mix well together;
put it into the prepared mould; let it set, and when firm dip in
warm water and turn out on a dish; place a compote of any kind
of fruit in the centre, cover the fruit over with lightly sweetened

whipped cream; garnish with cut angelica or dried cherries all around between the rice and the cream.

PUDDING IN SURPRISE A LA LOUISE

Line a charlotte mould thinly with lemon jelly, and ornament it with pieces of cut dried apricot, angelica, cherries, and little bunches of dried coconut, all of which are first set with a little lemon jelly; set the garnish to the mould with a little more jelly, and when this is firm line the mould with rum cream prepared as below; let this set, then fill up the mould with the pudding mixture prepared as below, and put the shape aside until the pudding is set; then dip it into hot water, and turn out the pudding on to a dish on a silver or gold dessert paper, and serve it for a sweet for dinner or luncheon.

RUM CREAM

Take a quarter of a pint of whipped cream, strain into it a quarter of a pint of lemon jelly in which four sheets of gelatine have been dissolved, colour with a few drops of carmine, flavour with half a wineglass of white rum, then use.

PUDDING MIXTURE

Boil half a pint of new milk with a split vanilla pod and two ounces of castor sugar; when sufficiently flavoured dissolve in it half an ounce of gelatine, and stir it all together with three raw

yolks of eggs that have been mixed together till smooth; stir over
the fire till thickening, then wring it through a clean tammy cloth,
and when beginning to set mix with it two and a half gills of
stiffly whipped cream, add half a wineglass of white rum, a
wineglassful of maraschino syrup, a good dust of ground cinnamon,
a quarter of a pound of cut dried fruits, one ounce of blanched
almonds, skinned, chopped, and baked a nice brown colour, and
three ounces of cut-up slices of sponge cake; stir carefully together
and then fill up the mould.

MALTAISE A LA CHANTILLY

Line a fancy jelly mould about one eighth of an inch thick with
lemon jelly, and when this is set, mask it over in equal divisions
with chocolate cream prepared as below, and white and pink
lemon cream prepared as below; let these set, then fill up the centre
of the mould with a purée of tangerine oranges and put it on ice
till set; dip the mould into hot water and turn out the shape on
to a dish; garnish it with stiffly whipped cream, and arrange on
this some chocolate varieties. Serve for a dinner or ball supper
dish.

PURÉE OF TANGERINES

Take eight tangerine oranges, the peels of which have been
rubbed over with three ounces of loaf sugar, and press the juice
and pulp from the fruit. Prepare one pint of lemon jelly with the
flavoured sugar and the usual other ingredients, using one ounce
of gelatine to the pint of water; reduce this pint of jelly to half a
pint by boiling it down, then let it cool somewhat, and add it to

the pulp of the oranges, then rub it all through a fine hair sieve with a few drops of apricot yellow and a tablespoonful of apricot jam, and add to it one wineglassful of maraschino, one wineglassful of white rum, and a quarter of a pint of stiffly whipped cream; mix together till quite smooth, then use.

LEMON CREAM

Three quarters of a pint of lemon jelly and one and a half gills of thick cream, flavour with vanilla essence, then divide into two parts; colour one part with a few drops of carmine, leave the other plain, and use as instructed.

CHOCOLATE CREAM

Take two ounces of powdered chocolate, and put it into a stewpan with half a pint of water and two ounces of icing sugar; let it boil on the side of the stove for fifteen minutes, then mix with not quite a quarter of an ounce of gelatine and a teaspoonful of vanilla essence; rub it through the tammy, put the mixture into the stewpan, and place it in the bain-marie till it has dissolved, then use.

FLAWN OF FRUITS, VIENNA FASHION

Line a channelled flawn-circle, or a hot-pie mould of shallow form, with tartlet-paste; adorn the crest of the borders with leaves of paste; egg these with the paste-brush, then mask the sides and bottom of the case with buttered paper; fill the hollow with dried kernels of cherries, or common flour; this being what is called cooking the crust *à blanc*. Push it into a moderate oven. Forty minutes after, take it out, empty, and let it cool, then mask it inside with a layer of apricot-marmalade. A quarter of an hour before serving, place the crust on a dish, fill its hollow with a *bavarois* preparation of rice and almond milk, thickened at the moment on ice, arranging it in layers, alternating with marmalade, and giving it a dome-like shape. Let the preparation get firm on ice for a few minutes, then surround it with a chain of greengages, and another of halves of peaches, prepared as for compote; garnish the hollow with a group of cooked cherries, or raw strawberries; mask the fruits, with the paste-brush, in their own syrup, being cold, mixed up with the juice of apples, and reduced to a nicety.

This *entremets* is not only one of the prettiest, but moreover is excellent, and luxurious.

LEMON CHEESECAKES
TO KEEP SEVERAL YEARS

A quarter of a pound of butter; one pound of loaf sugar; six eggs; the peel of two lemons, the juice of three.

To a quarter of a pound of butter put a pound of loaf sugar, broken into lumps, six eggs well beaten, leaving out two whites, the peel of two lemons grated, and the juice of three. Put all into a nice brass pan, and let it simmer over the fire till it is dissolved and begins to look like honey, then pour it into jars, and tie it down tightly with bladders. Keep it in a dry place. When you use it, have ready some very small tins, make a good puff paste, and fill them *half* full with cheesecakes, as they will rise very much. When cold, add a little grated sugar.

NB: It must be stirred gently all the time it is on the fire.

BURNT CREAM

One pint of cream; peel of half a lemon; a stick of cinnamon; one ounce and a half of sugar; yolks of four eggs.

Boil a pint of cream with the peel of the lemon and the stick of cinnamon. Take it off the fire, and pour it very slowly on the well-beaten yolks of the four eggs, stirring till half cold; add the sugar pounded and sifted. Take out the spice and lemon peel; pour it into a dish, and when cold strew over it some pounded sugar, and brown it with a salamander.

FLUMMERY

One ounce of sweet and one of bitter almonds; one pint of calf's-feet stock; sugar to taste; one pint of cream; a little orange-flower water.

Blanch one ounce of bitter and one ounce of sweet almonds, and beat them in a mortar with a little orange-flower water to keep them from oiling. Put them into a pint of calf's-foot stock, set it over the fire, and sweeten it to your taste. As soon as it boils, strain it through a piece of muslin, and when it is quite cool, put it into a pint of thick cream, and keep stirring it often till it becomes thick and cold. Then pour it into a mould which has been oiled or laid in cold water. Let it stand six or seven hours before you turn it out, as if very stiff it will greatly improve the appearance of the flummery, and it will turn out without putting the mould in hot water, which will give a dullness to the flummery.

LARGE PEAR, FARCED

Get a large pear, *duchesse* or *beurre*, not too ripe. Peel it, leaving a piece of the stalk adhering; cut the pear transversally about two-thirds of its height (on the side of the stalk), empty the thicker part by aid of a vegetable-spoon. Boil the two parts of the pear in water, keeping the pieces rather firm; allow them to cool in the syrup, then drain them on a cloth. Now place the lower part of the pear on a layer of rice with cream, which is cold, and ranged on a dish. Fill the interior of the pear with a salpicon of fruits, thickened with a little apricot-marmalade, or jelly; cover it with the other piece of pear, and surround the whole, at its base, with a circle of greengages, over which, as well as over the pear itself, pour a little syrup reduced with vanilla.

PEACH-TARTLETS

Spread a dozen tartlet-moulds with the prepared paste, mask the bottom with a thin layer of apple-marmalade, and fill to half their height with rice boiled in milk. Bake them, covered with paper, in the oven. Ten minutes after having been taken out of the oven, mask the bottom with another thin layer of marmalade, fill the empty space with good rice, finished with cream; on which rice place half a peach, cooked as for compote, but kept firm, and cut out with a tin-cutter, to give it a round shape. Now surround the peaches with a chain of meringue-beads, squeezed between the paste and the peaches; sprinkle over sugar, keep the tartlets at the mouth of the oven for ten or twelve minutes; when taken out, mask the peaches, by aid of a paste-brush, with their syrup reduced to a glaze; dish the tartlets, in a group, on a folded napkin.

TARTLET-PASTE

Pass a pound of flour through a sieve on a table, form a hollow in its centre, and into this hollow put three-quarters of a pound of butter broken into small bits, three yolks of eggs, a little salt, two tablespoonfuls of powder-sugar, as well as a little cold water; mix gradually into the flour the butter and liquid, thus forming a smooth paste, but without working too much.

RICH APPLE PUDDING

One pound of apples; half a pound of sugar; six eggs; one lemon; a quarter of a pound of butter; puff paste.

Pare and core a pound of apples, put them into a stewpan with sufficient water to prevent their burning, and stew them till they will pulp; then add to them the sugar pounded, the rind of the lemon grated, and six well-beaten eggs. Stir all well together, and just before putting it into the oven, melt the butter and stir it into the other ingredients. Put a puff paste round a pie-dish, pour in the pudding, and bake it.

DUKE OF CLARENCE'S PUDDING

Half a pound of sultana raisins; one French roll; one glass of brandy; one of white wine; four eggs; one pint of milk; two ounces of citron; and a little sugar.

Take a basin that will hold rather more than a pint, butter it well, and flour it, after that turn the basin up to shake off any loose flour; stick some raisins in various devices over it, up to the top. Take a French roll, without the crust, grate it, strew it thin and lightly over the raisins, then slices of citron and fruit alternately, with a glass of brandy and white wine poured over it. Well beat four eggs, and stir them into a pint of milk, with sugar to your taste, pour it by degrees into the basin on the other ingredients, and let it stand one hour. Then dip the pudding cloth into boiling water, put the basin carefully into it, tie closely down, and boil it one hour.

CHRISTMAS PLUM PUDDING

One pound and a half of raisins; half a pound of currants; three quarters of a pound of breadcrumbs; half a pound of flour; three quarters of a pound of beef suet; nine eggs; one wineglass of brandy; half a pound of citron and orange peel; half a nutmeg; and a little ground ginger.

Chop the suet as fine as possible, and mix it with the breadcrumbs and the flour; add the currants washed and dried, the citron and orange peel cut into thin slices, and the raisins stoned and divided. Mix it all well together with the grated nutmeg and ginger, then stir in nine eggs well beaten, and the brandy, and again mix it thoroughly together that every ingredient may be moistened; put it into a buttered mould, tie it over tightly, and boil it for six hours. Serve it ornamented with holly, and brandy poured round it.

This pudding may be made a month before using, boiled in a cloth, and hung up in a dry place, and when required put into a saucepan of boiling water and boiled for two hours or two hours and a half, then turned out, and served with sauce as above.

POTATO PUDDING

Half a pound of potatoes; half a pound of sugar; half a pound of butter; five eggs; peel and juice of a lemon.

Boil some mealy potatoes and press them through a sieve. Then add to them the pounded sugar, the butter beaten to a cream, the peel of the lemon grated, and the juice with five eggs well beaten. Mix all thoroughly together, put it into a dish, and bake it in a quick oven.

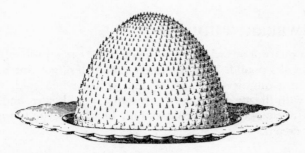

ENGLISH TIPSY-PUDDING

Prepare a paste with half a pound of sugar, four whole eggs, two yolks of eggs, three whites of eggs well whipped, nearly half a pound of butter, a quarter of a pound of flour, a little salt, a little grated zest.

Butter and flour a dome-shaped mould; which flour, and fill with the previously prepared paste; cover it, wrap it up in a cloth, plunge it into boiling water, and let it continue for full two hours. When about to serve, drain the mould, turn the pudding out on a dish; pour over it as much warm Madeira as it will imbibe; mask it, by aid of a paste-brush, with apricot-marmalade, stick its surface all over with fillets of blanched almonds, dried in the oven.

ORANGE TARTLETS

Two Seville oranges; a piece of butter the size of a walnut; twice the weight of the oranges in pounded sugar; puff paste.

Take out the pulp from two Seville oranges, boil the peels until quite tender, and then beat them to a paste with twice their weight in pounded loaf sugar; then add the pulp and the juice of the oranges with a piece of butter the size of a walnut, beat all these ingredients well together, line some patty-pans with a rich puff paste, lay the orange mixture in them, and bake them.

STRAWBERRY PUDDING

Mash a quart of strawberries with sugar to taste – probably three-quarters of a pound. Melt an ounce and a half of gelatine in rather less than a tumblerful of hot water, which, when cold, is to be mixed with the strawberries. Put it into a mould, surround it with ice till it sets and gets as cold as may be. Turn it out, and serve it with cream.

PRINCE'S PUDDING

Have roasted in a pan about half a pound of coffee-berries; as it gives out the moisture, pour into it three gills of boiling milk, kept beside the fire; cover the stewpan, take it off the fire, and allow the infusion to cool. Put into a kitchen-basin ten or twelve yolks of eggs; which whip, and dilute with the infusion passed through a sieve; add sugar, and seven or eight leaves of dissolved gelatine.

Put into another basin a quarter of a pound of well cleansed and picked Smyrna raisins, as well as eighteen candied or syrup-chestnuts, each of which must be divided into three pieces; add three tablespoonfuls of pistachios cut in dice; which fruits baste with half a gill of kirsch.

Split in two lengthwise fifteen finger-biscuits, cut them again transversally, thus forming little squares; which keep on a plate.

Surround a large cylindric dome-shaped mould with pounded ice, adorn its base, and the upper part of its interior sides, with rounds of angelica, dipped one by one in half-set jelly; adorn its centre with a circle, composed of small raisins and preserved fruits; then spread the hollow of the mould with a small part of the previously prepared cream; thicken the remainder on the ice; when well set, add to it the fruits, and take it off. Now take it up with a spoon, fill the hollow of the mould, alternating each layer of the preparation with one of the biscuits cut in dice, and soaked with kirsch.

One hour after, dip the mould in hot water, wipe it well, and turn the pudding out on a dish, having fixed to its centre a small support of fried bread, masked with marmalade. Into this bread insert six hâtélet skewers, garnished with fruits, the largest of which is put in the centre. Send up separately a sauceboatful of English-cream, flavoured with coffee, and cooled on the ice.

PLUM PUDDING

INGREDIENTS

One and three quarter pounds of chopped beef suet, three quarters of a pound of freshly made white breadcrumbs, six ounces of flour, a quarter of a pound of cornflour, three quarters of a pound of stoned raisins, a quarter of a pound of chopped almonds, three quarters of a pound of currants washed and dried, three quarters of a pound of sultanas, one pound of chopped apples, half a pound of chopped mixed peel, one pound of moist sugar, the juice of two lemons, the peel of two lemons cut fine and chopped, one nutmeg grated, half a pound of crême de riz, two wineglasses of white rum, half a pint of milk, six whole eggs, and two ounces of baking powder.

Mix these ingredients well together in a basin, then tie them up tightly in a clean pudding-cloth that is dusted over with flour and brown sugar, put into boiling water, and boil for about twelve hours. The pudding may also be boiled in a basin, in which case the basin should be buttered and then dusted over inside with demerara sugar and the ingredients put in and a cloth tied over. When the pudding is cooked, turn it out, dust it over with a little castor sugar, and serve brandy or white rum butter with it.

PLUM PUDDING [*richer*]

INGREDIENTS

Two and a half pounds of chopped beef suet, half a pound of freshly made white breadcrumbs, three quarters of a pound of dried cherries, six ounces of fine flour, one pound of stoned raisins chopped, one pound of picked sultanas, one pound of currants washed and dried, half a pound of almonds chopped, one and a half pounds of moist sugar, one pound of mixed peel chopped, one and a half pounds of chopped apples, a quarter of a pound of cornflour, ten eggs, the juice and chopped peel of four lemons, one grated nutmeg, half a pound of crême de riz, two ounces of baking powder, one wineglass of brandy, two wineglasses of white rum, a quarter of a pint of milk, and a saltspoonful of salt.

Mix, cook in a mould, basin or cloth, and serve as in previous recipe.

SAUCES,
GARNISHES
&
PICKLES

BROWN SAUCE

Two ounces of butter; two pounds of beef; two onions; a quarter
of a pound of lean bacon; two cloves; one bayleaf; pepper; salt;
and two quarts of water.

Put two ounces of butter at the bottom of a stewpan with the
bacon cut into small bits, and the beef into very thin slices, with
two small onions, a little pepper, salt, cloves, bayleaf, and a very
little water to prevent its burning; stir it over the fire for ten
or twelve minutes, then let it simmer until it looks brown and rich;
fill up the stewpan with two quarts of water, and when boiling set
it at the corner, skim off every particle of fat, and let it simmer
slowly for an hour and a half; when done strain it through a sieve.

A FAMILY COULIS

Two ounces of butter rolled in flour; one pint of broth; half a
pint of good gravy; a glass of white wine; a bunch of sweet herbs;
two cloves; a little nutmeg and mace; six mushrooms; pepper and
salt.

Roll about two ounces of butter in a little flour, and stir it over a slow fire in a stewpan until the flour is a yellow colour, then pour in a pint of thin broth, half a pint of good gravy, and a glass of white wine; add a bunch of sweet herbs, two cloves, a little nutmeg and mace, six mushrooms if you have them, and a little pepper and salt; let it stew for an hour over a slow fire; take off all the scum, and strain it through a fine hair sieve for use.

A RICH GRAVY

Six ounces of lean ham or bacon; two pounds of gravy beef; one large onion, or two shallots; five pints of water; four cloves; one blade of mace; thirty peppercorns; a bunch of savoury herbs; half a head of celery; one carrot; salt; one tablespoonful of mushroom ketchup; one of cayenne vinegar.

Cut about six ounces of bacon or ham into very small pieces, and brown them in a little butter. Dredge with a little pepper and flour the two pounds of beef, and slightly fry it. Put the bacon at the bottom of the stewpan with the beef on the top; then the onion or shallot also browned, and pour in five pints of water; bring it gently to the boil; skim it clean; add a blade of mace, four cloves, thirty peppercorns, a bunch of savoury herbs, half a head of celery sliced, one carrot, and a little salt. Boil all together till reduced to half the quantity of gravy; strain it, and when cold take off the cake of fat, warm it again in your stewpan, add a tablespoonful of walnut ketchup, the same of cayenne vinegar, and if required, a piece of butter rolled in flour to thicken it. Half this quantity can be made.

FISH SAUCE TO KEEP

Twenty-four anchovies; four shallots; three dessertspoonfuls of horseradish; eight blades of mace; twelve cloves; two lemons; half a pint of anchovy liquor; a quart of hock; a pint of water; three tablespoonfuls of walnut ketchup.

Slice the lemons, chop the anchovies up with the shallots, scrape the horseradish fine. Mix all the ingredients. Boil it till it is reduced to a quart. Strain it off, and when it is cold bottle it, and put it away in small bottles closely corked down and sealed, for use. We generally add the walnut ketchup when the sauce has become cold, instead of boiling it with the other ingredients.

A small quantity, added to melted butter while making, will at any time make a nice fish sauce.

BÉCHAMEL SAUCE

Half a pound of ham; a pound and a quarter of veal; one small onion; three shallots; three blades of mace; a head of celery; a bunch of sweet herbs; three mushrooms; half a pint of veal broth or water; rather more than a quart of milk; a little cayenne; salt.

Shred half a pound of lean ham very fine, put it at the bottom of a stewpan; lay on it a pound and a quarter of lean veal cut small, an onion cut into rings, three shallots sliced small, the white part of a head of celery, a bunch of sweet herbs, three blades of mace, and three mushrooms cut up and placed on the meat. Pour in half a pint of veal broth or water, cover it close, put it over a slow fire, and let it simmer gently for half an hour, taking care it does not stick to the pan, or burn; then add nearly a quart of new milk; stir it round, and stew it slowly for half an hour; thicken it with two teaspoonfuls of flour mixed smoothly in a little milk and stirred gradually in, adding a little cayenne and salt to your taste; let it stew till sufficiently rich, then strain it through a sieve, and it will be ready for use.

SAUCE FOR A ROAST PIG

One glass of port wine; five cloves; a quarter of a pint of breadcrumbs; one ounce of butter; a little flour; one ounce of currants; one large cupful of water.

Boil an ounce of currants for about seven or eight minutes in a large cupful of water; then pour it boiling over a quarter of a pint of breadcrumbs, and let them soak for some little time. Then stir in an ounce of butter, with a little flour, five cloves, and a glass of port wine; stir it over the fire until it is a fine smooth sauce, and serve with venison or roasted pig.

CELERY SAUCE

For poultry or game. Slice very thin four or five heads of celery, and put into a saucepan with pepper, salt, a pinch of sugar, a sliced onion, and for every head of celery an ounce of butter. Let it stew very slowly till the celery is melted; only take care not to brown it. Then add four ounces of flour, with about a pint of milk; let it cook for twenty minutes more, and rub it through a sieve. Pureé of celery is the same as the foregoing, but thicker. Use more celery and less milk. Finish it with a pat of butter, and serve it as a garnish for cutlets.

OYSTER SAUCE

Boil two dozen oysters very gently in their own liquor for five minutes, always remembering that quick boiling will harden them; then drain them and beard them. Go through the first step of making English sauce, using the liquor of the oysters (strained, of course) instead of water, and adding an equal quantity of milk. Put in the oysters, heat up the sauce, and lastly melt into it – but no more than melt – an ounce of butter. For a broiled beefsteak it is preferable to use good brown gravy instead of the milk.

POTTED CRAYFISH

One hundred and fifty crayfish; three ounces of fresh butter; pepper; salt; and mace.

Pick out the meat from the boiled crayfish, and pound them in a mortar with the butter to a paste, seasoning them at the same time with the pounded mace, salt, and pepper. Put the paste into pots, pour over it clarified butter, and tie it closely over to exclude the air, and to prevent it from spoiling.

ADMIRAL ROSS'S INDIAN DEVIL MIXTURE

Four tablespoonfuls of cold gravy; one of chutney paste; one of ketchup; one of vinegar; two teaspoonfuls of made mustard; two of salt; two tablespoonfuls of butter.

Mix all the above ingredients as smooth as possible in a soup plate, put with it the cold meat, or whatever you wish to devil. Stew it gently until thoroughly warmed, and then you will have a good devil.

GARNISH A LA FINANCIÈRE

Three cockscombs; three fat livers; three lambs' sweetbreads; six quenelles; five artichoke bottoms; six truffles; six mushrooms.

This extravagant garnish belongs so entirely to first-rate cooks who know their business entirely, that we need scarcely give a receipt for it, as in ordinary kitchens it is never required.

The cockscombs are prepared by steeping them in boiling water, drying them, and rubbing off the skin. They require soaking for several hours to blanch. Then they are dried and stewed in butter, lemon juice, and a little salt, moistening them with some stock. Livers and lambs' sweetbreads are soaked, blanched, and added when the cockscombs are boiling; bottoms of artichokes, sliced truffles, and mushrooms are added when the other ingredients are almost cooked.

LEMON PICKLE

Six lemons, cut or scored into four parts, not quite through the rind; fill the incisions and cover the lemons with salt for a week, then take them out, clear them from the salt, put them into a jar with good vinegar, a very little saffron, mace, and one clove; cover them completely with the vinegar, put a plate or cover on the jar, and stew the lemons about three hours, or till tender, in a slow oven. Then remove them, add some fresh vinegar to the other vinegar, and boil some white peppercorns and cayenne in it. Cut the lemons into eight pieces, pour the vinegar over them, and tie them up. A little of the liquid is good for white sauce, etc.

DRINKS

CARDINAL BOWL, WITH STRAWBERRIES

Grate the zest of an orange on a piece of loaf-sugar, weighing two
or three ounces; put it into a glass or china vessel with ten ounces
of cut sugar; moisten with a little cold water, and the juice of five
oranges passed through a sieve; the sugar melted, add to it a bottle
of good Moselle wine, and a little rum; plunge into the beverage
a handful of fresh strawberries, then place this in a glass vessel,
and keep it on the ice for full an hour.

When about to serve, place the vessel on a tray, surround it
with glasses, and serve, in the conditions shown by the drawing.

STRAWBERRY SHERBET

One pound of strawberries; three pints of water; juice of one
lemon; one tablespoonful of orange-flower water; one pound of
double-refined sugar.

Take one pound of picked strawberries, crush them to a smooth
mass; then add three pints of water, the juice of a lemon, and a
tablespoonful of orange-flower water; let it stand for three or

four hours. Put a pound of double-refined sugar into another basin, stretch over it a large cloth or napkin, and strain the strawberries through it on the sugar, wring it to extract as much of the juice as possible; stir until the sugar is dissolved, then strain again, and set it in ice for an hour before serving, in small tumblers.

LEMON BRANDY

Three quarts of brandy; a pound and three-quarters of loaf sugar; peel of six lemons; juice of twelve; one quart of boiling milk.

Take three quarts of the best brandy, put it in a jar, or a pan, with a cover, and add to it a pound and three-quarters of loaf sugar, the peel of six lemons cut *very* thin, and the juice of twelve, strained from the seeds; pour over it very gradually a quart of boiling milk, let it stand eight days, stirring it every day, then strain it through a flannel bag and bottle it for use.

EXCELLENT ENGLISH SHERRY

Thirty pounds of good moist sugar; ten gallons of water; eight quarts of ale; six pounds of raisins; one quart of brandy; one pound of brown sugar candy; two ounces of isinglass.

Put to thirty pounds of good moist sugar ten gallons of water. Boil it half an hour, skim it well, and then let it stand till quite cold. Add eight quarts of ale from the ale vat while fermenting, stir it well together, let it remain in the tub till next day; then put it into the barrel with six pounds of raisins, one quart of brandy, one pound of brown sugarcandy and two ounces of isinglass. Let it remain three weeks before the barrel is closed, and it must stand twelve months before it is put into bottles.

SUPERIOR GINGER WINE

One pound of Jamaica ginger; fifty-six pounds of loaf sugar; six dozen lemons; two bottles of brandy; eighteen gallons of water; two tablespoonfuls of new yeast.

Take the best Jamaica ginger, slice it very thin, and tie it in a cloth. Boil it with the sugar and the water for three-quarters of an hour, skimming it all the time. Pare the lemons very thin, and pour the boiling liquor over the peels. Let it stand until the next day, then stir in the juice of the lemons, and put it into the cask with the ginger and the yeast. Stir all together, and let it stand till it has done working. Then add the brandy, and bung it up close. It will be fit to bottle in three months.

MOCK CHAMPAGNE

To every quart of grapes, one quart of water; to every gallon of juice, allow three pounds of loaf sugar; half an ounce of isinglass to every ten gallons of wine, and a quart of brandy to every five gallons.

Pick the grapes when full grown and just beginning to change colour, bruise them in a tub, pour in the water, and let them stand for three days, stirring once each day; then press the fruit through a cloth, let it stand for three or four hours, pour it carefully from any sediment, and add to it the sugar. Barrel it, and put the bung slightly in; at the end of three weeks, or when it has done working, put in the isinglass, previously dissolved in some of the liquor. Stir it for three days once a day, and at the last stirring add the brandy. In three or four days bung it down close, and in six months it should be bottled, and the corks tied down, or wired.

CLARET CUP

One bottle of claret; one bottle of soda-water; one glass of brandy or sherry; one strip of cucumber; peel of half a lemon; sugar to your taste; a large lump of ice.

Put all the above ingredients into a silver cup, pass a napkin through one of the handles, that the edge of the cup may be wiped after the contents have been partaken of, and hand it round to each person.

SUPERIOR CLARET CUP

Two bottles of claret; one of champagne; three glasses of sherry; one of noyau; half a pound of ice; one sprig of borage, or a few slices of cucumber; sugar, if required.

Mix and serve as above.

EGG FLIP

Three eggs; a quarter of a pound of good moist sugar; a pint and a half of beer.

Beat three whole eggs with a quarter of a pound of good moist sugar; make a pint and a half of beer very hot, but do not let it boil, then mix it gradually with the beaten eggs and sugar, toss it to and fro from the saucepan into a jug two or three times, grate a little nutmeg on the top and serve it.

A wineglass of spirits may be added if liked.

EGG WINE

One glass of white wine; one spoonful of cold water; a few lumps of loaf sugar; a little grated nutmeg; one egg.

Put a glass of white wine with half a wineglass of cold water, a little sugar, and grated nutmeg, into a very clean saucepan; set it over the fire, and when it boils pour it by degrees over an egg well beaten with a spoonful of cold water, stir it one way for a minute, and serve it with dry toast in a plate.

MULLED EGGS

Beat the yolk of a recently laid egg; stir to it a little milk or cream; then pour to it more hot milk or hot coffee, tea, water, ale or wine, stirring it well all the time. If the hot liquid be added too hastily, or without being well stirred, the egg will coagulate or curdle instead of uniting with the fluid. Sugar or flavouring may be added according to taste.

MULLED WINE

One quart of new milk; one stick of cinnamon; nutmeg; and sugar to taste; yolks of six eggs; a spoonful or two of cream.

Boil a quart of new milk five minutes with a stick of cinnamon, nutmeg and sugar to your taste, then take it off the fire and let it cool. Beat the yolks of six eggs very well, and mix them with a large spoonful or two of cold cream, then mix it with the wine, and pour it backwards and forwards from the saucepan to the jug several times.

Send it to table with biscuits.

MILK PUNCH

Over the zest of four lemons and a Seville orange pour a pint of rum; cover it up, and let it stand for twelve hours. Then strain it, and mix it with another pint of rum, a pint of brandy, a pint of sherry, half a pint of lemon juice, a pineapple peeled, sliced and pounded, a pint of green tea, a grated nutmeg, a pound of dissolved sugar, the whites of two eggs frothed, two pints of boiling water and two of boiling milk. Mix it well, let it stand for a little time, strain it through a beaver jelly-bag, and bottle it. To be served after turtle soup.

GLOSSARY

Aspic cream: A mixture of semi-liquid aspic jelly and mayonnaise or fresh double cream.

Aspic jelly: A savoury gelatine, prepared at home from calf's-foot stock, isinglass and various flavourings, but also available commercially. Used widely for garnishing cold dishes, and in semi-liquid form for glazing and setting same.

Bain-marie: A large square or oblong tin capable of holding a number of smaller containers. Filled with hot water and placed on the hearth or the range, it keeps vessels holding sauces, soups, etc., at an even temperature without further cooking or thickening of the contents.

Bard, to: A substitute for larding (*q.v.*). The bard is a thin slice of bacon fat placed over the breasts of poultry or game to prevent their drying out while cooking.

Blanch, to: Of meat and vegetables, to place in cold water which is then brought to the boil; the material being blanched is then drained and rinsed in cold water. The process tenderises vegetables and removes any scum from meat. Of almonds, to plunge into boiling water in order to remove the skins.

Braise, to: 'A mode of cooking by the action of heat *above*, as well as *below*, the article cooked.' A braising-pan proper has a deep cover on which live charcoal is placed. The pan itself should be air-tight, so that the food within absorbs all the flavour. Cooking itself is done very slowly.

Broth, white: A stock made from white meat, e.g. chicken or veal.

Carmine: Cochineal or other red food colouring.

Caul of pork: The peritoneum, a sheet of fatty membrane which encloses the stomach and intestines of the pig. Still used in French *charcuterie* instead of larding. Fat bacon may be used as a substitute.

Coquille: Scallop-shell or china or metal dish in that shape.

Cornet: Flexible cone-shaped bag of the type still used by confectioners in cake-decoration. Also called a farcing or forcing bag.

Coulis or cullis: A rich brown gravy.

Couronne, en: To serve any article (e.g. cutlets, fritters) with one overlapping the other in a crown or ring.

Court-bouillon: A type of stock, used especially in the cooking of fish. For ingredients see *Slice of Salmon with Montpellier Butter* (p. 45).

Crême de riz: Rice cream. A commercial preparation used to give body to soups, and in cakes, custards, etc. Probably composed of rice cooked in milk and then pounded to a fine paste.

Croustade: See *pain-vert*.

Duxelles, faggot of: A bouquet garni of bayleaf, chives and mushrooms.

Egg-balls: A type of gnocchi or farfel served in soup.

Farce, forcemeat: A finely chopped and pounded mixture of meat (cooked or raw) or fish and flavourings (e.g. herbs, wine, ketchup) used as a garnish when piped through a forcing-bag or cornet (*q.v.*), in quenelles (*q.v.*), and as a stuffing for game, poultry and fish.

Financière: Name of an ornate sauce and of a type of garnish: for ingredients see *Calf's Head à la Financière* (p.61), and page 121 in the section on *Sauces*.

Flour, baked: Flour placed in a hot oven and baked until a light tan colour.

Flour, dried: As above, but removed before the flour has begun to colour. Both processes make the flour less likely to 'lump' when added as thickening or used in cake-making.

Galantine: Meat or poultry boned and stuffed with forcemeat, truffles, etc., braised or boiled, and served cold, with aspic jelly.

Glacé: In cakemaking, thin water icing; also icecream.

Glaze: Usually meat, but occasionally fish, stock which has been reduced by boiling to a thick sauce or jelly; used to give meat or fish an attractive shine before its presentation at table, and also as concentrated stock. If a meat glaze is called for, a meat extract such as Bovril may be substituted.

Ham, essence of: A ham flavoured liquor, as in anchovy essence. Substitute a finely-chopped slice of a raw ham such as Westphalia or Parma.

Hâtélet skewer: Type of skewer with ornamented head used in serving dishes to table, partly as decoration and partly to fix the meat, poultry, etc., to its base. Usually silver or silver plate.

Herbs, bunch of, sweet, pot: Variants of bouquet garni, i.e. thyme, bay-leaf, parsley, marjoram, basil.

Herbs, savoury: Sage, rosemary, thyme, and if a fish dish, fennel.

Ketchup, mushroom: Usually home-made, but the most widely-used commercial preparation of the period, Burgess's, is still available. Use also as a substitute for mushroom powder.

Lard, to: To pass fat (usually bacon-fat) through the skin of a bird or the surface of a piece of meat before roasting, so as to provide a constant baste and prevent the meat's drying out in cooking. A special hollow needle (larding-needle) is used.

Leason or liaison: Yolk of egg beaten smooth with cream and added, just before serving, to some soups and sauces to thicken them. Also used, more rarely, of oil and vinegar combined as a salad dressing.

Lobster coral: Lobster spawn; rather like hard cod's roe, but with less flavour. Used as a garnish and, pounded, in dishes to give an orange-pink colour. Substitute a little paprika.

Marinade: A type of pickle, consisting usually of oil and vinegar or lemon juice (sometimes red wine) and seasoning, e.g. thyme, bayleaf, peppercorns, in which meat, and occasionally fish, is steeped before cooking. It tenderises meat and sharpens the flavour of whatever is marinaded.

Mask, to: To cover thinly with a layer of forcemeat, unset aspic, mayonnaise, etc.

Meat extract: Substitute for glaze. Use Bovril or Marmite.

Minion-fillets: Small fillets from the breast of a chicken.

Mirepoix: A highly-flavoured and concentrated sauce consisting of wine, root vegetables, onions, celery leaves and spices, used with entrées.

Mustard, flour of: Unprepared English mustard powder.

Onion, black: An onion which has been placed in a hot oven and roasted until black. Used in stews, etc., to give flavour and colour.

Pain-vert: A case or platter made of pastry, fried bread, forcemeat etc., used as an edible base for ornamental dishes; for a typical pastry recipe see *Turban of Rabbit à la Pluche* (p.64). Also called a *croustade*.

Panard, panada: A mixture of butter, flour, water and salt, slowly cooked. Pounded, an ingredient in most forcemeats.

Pass, to: To sauté, usually in butter, without browning.

Paste: Pastry.

Paste, Nouille: 'Mix three or four raw yolks of eggs into half a pound of fine flour, add a saltspoonful of salt and a good dust of coralline pepper, and work it into a stiff paste with cold water, roll out thin and use.'

Paste-brush: Pastry-brush.

Paste, raised: See recipe for *Salmon Pie Raised* (p. 101). Also known as hot-water paste.

Paste, suet: See recipe for *Small Raised Yorkshire Pork Pies.*

Pepper, coralline: A mixture of cayenne and paprika.

Pepper, mignonette: White or black pepper, coarsely ground.

Poach, to: To boil or cook gently in water or stock.

Poularde: A small, young chicken weighing between $2\frac{1}{4}$ and $2\frac{3}{4}$lb. Also called a *poulet*.

Quenelle: An oval of forcemeat or savoury mixture used in garnishing. Can be made with a special implement, or by using two dessert-spoons as a mould. *Quenelle forcemeat* is a finely-pounded forcemeat the base of which is always veal, lamb or other white meat.

Raspings: Hard breadcrumbs, so called because of their method of preparation, i.e. toasting bread until crisp and then rasping it into crumbs on a grater.

Reduce, to: Process of rapidly boiling stock or sauces in order to concentrate flavour, or to thicken without the addition of flour.

Refresh, to: To plunge in cold water.

Remove back, to: To set a pan at the back of the range (which was of course kept burning all day); i.e. to remove a dish or pan from direct heat and allow its contents to finish cooking very slowly.

Roast, to: To cook before or over an open fire on a spit or jack. Victorian cookery makes a strong distinction, as we do not, between roasting proper, and *baking*, which is carried out in an enclosed oven.

Roux: Butter and flour worked into a paste and used for thickening. The basis also for roux-sauce, which was prepared by the addition of milk to the roux over heat.

Salamander: A type of kitchen utensil, consisting of an iron grid or slab with a handle. The grid was heated red-hot and then held or passed several times over the surface of a dish which was to be browned. Used when the oven was not hot enough, or if baking was undesirable for the dish as a whole.

Salpicon: A mixture, the ingredients of which are usually specified, e.g. a salpicon of game or of fruits.

Sauces

BÉCHAMEL: See p. 119 in *Sauces* section.

BROWN: See p. 117 in *Sauces* section. Also known as *chaudfroid.*

CRUET: A sauce composed of the several ingredients of the cruet, combined according to taste – i.e. salt, pepper, mustard, vinegar, and occasionally oil. A type of vinaigrette dressing.

ENGLISH: White or roux sauce, i.e. butter, flour, water and milk.

FINANCIÈRE: See p. 121 in *Sauces* section.

PIQUANTE: See recipe for *Fried Ox Ears* (pp. 51-2).

REFORME: See recipe for *Epigrams of Mutton à la Reitz* (p. 67).

VELOUTÉ: See recipe for *Little Bombes of Veal à la Gelée* (p. 63).

SPANISH: Brown sauce plus ham or bacon. Also called *Espagnol.*

Sippets: Croûtons of fried bread.

Tammy: A fine cloth strainer, usually of muslin or woollen canvas, used for extracting fruit juice from pulp, making a very fine purée, etc.

Trail: The intestines of two small game birds, the snipe and the woodcock; always served with, and often still inside, the bird, these species being supposed to live on an exclusively vegetable diet and their intestines therefore fit for consumption.

Truffles: Edible, highly aromatic subterranean fungi found at certain times of the year in parts of France and Italy. Rarely to be purchased fresh in Britain now, but still obtainable tinned, at great expense.

Warm-closet: A movable cupboard placed before the kitchen range, designed to keep plates and finished dishes warm.

Zest: The thinly-pared rind of a lemon or orange.